Helicopter Maneuvers
Manual
A step-by-step illustrated guide to performing all helicopter flight operations

Ryan Dale

AVIATION SUPPLIES & ACADEMICS
NEWCASTLE, WASHINGTON

Helicopter Maneuvers Manual
by Ryan Dale

Aviation Supplies & Academics, Inc.
7005 132nd Place SE
Newcastle, Washington 98059-3153

Visit the ASA website often (www.asa2fly.com, Product Updates) to find updates posted there due to FAA regulation, policy, or procedure changes that may affect this book.

Illustrations based on the author's original drawings.
Cover photo: Robinson Helicopter Company

ASA-HELI-FM
ISBN 978-1-56027-891-7

Printed in the United States of America
2022   2021   2020   2019   9   8   7   6   5   4

Library of Congress Cataloging-in-Publication Data

Dale, Ryan.
   Helicopter maneuvers manual : step-by-step guide to performing all
helicopter flight operations / Ryan Dale. — 1st ed.
      p. cm.
   ISBN 9781560278917 (trade paper) — ISBN 1560278919 (trade paper)
   1. Helicopters — Piloting — Handbooks, manuals, etc. I. Title.
   TL716.5.D348 2011
   629.132'5252—dc23
                              2011042350

06

Contents

Introduction

The purpose of this book is to help new pilots visualize each flight maneuver before ever stepping into the helicopter, and to provide flight instructors with a resource to help transfer knowledge to the student. I've spent many hours drawing maneuvers on the whiteboard to help illustrate exactly what to do or expect at each point in a maneuver. This repetition and my lack of freehand drawing skills motivated me to sit down and write a clear, concise definition with detailed illustrations for each maneuver in the helicopter Practical Test Standards (PTS).

Included in this guide are all the maneuvers required for the private and commercial checkride with detailed explanations to help visualize the maneuvers step-by-step. I have also included practical tips for both students and instructors, covering common errors and ways to accelerate the learning process. The advantage of this book is that it can be used with all makes and models of helicopters. I've also included specific tips for the popular Robinson R22 helicopter.

—Ryan Dale

The following acronyms and terms are used throughout this book.

A/FD—Airport/Facility Directory
AGL—above ground level
CAT—carburetor air temperature
CG—center of gravity
ETL—effective translational lift
KIAS—knots indicated airspeed
LMP—limit manifold pressure
MAP—manifold air pressure
MCP—maximum continuous power
MEL—minimum equipment list
M/R—main rotor

OGE—out of ground effect
P/C links—pitch change links
PIC—pilot-in-command
POH—Pilot's Operating Handbook
PTS—Practical Test Standards
RFM—Rotorcraft Flight Manual
RPM—revolutions per minute
T/R—tail rotor
VSI—vertical speed indicator
V_Y—best rate-of-climb speed

abeam. On a line at a right angle to the aircraft.

anti-torque pedal. Located under your feet, these pedals change the pitch of the tail rotor that counteracts the torque of the main rotor.

attitude. Synonymous with pitch of the helicopter.

backside of power curve. Because of the "U" shape of the lift/drag graph, the slower the helicopter is, the more power is required maintaining altitude.

collective. Located at your left hand, this collectively changes the pitch of all the main rotor blades.

(Continued)

Coriolis effect. The force acting perpendicular to the direction of motion and to the axis of rotation.

correlator. A mechanical linkage that opens the throttle when the collective is raised, and closes the throttle when the collective is lowered.

crab. Occurs when the heading of the helicopter does not match the ground track due to wind.

cyclic. Located at your right hand, this changes the pitch of the main rotor blade in its plane of rotation.

detent. A mechanical catch that allows the collective to be raised or lowered, and that will override the correlator so as to not open the throttle.

dynamic rollover. The lateral rolling tendency of the helicopter when one wheel or skid is stuck while the helicopter is attempting to hover.

leeward. The backside of an obstacle that faces away from the wind.

rotor mast. The part of the helicopter between the main rotor and the rest of the helicopter.

slip. Ignoring wind and aligning the heading of the helicopter to the ground track.

translating tendency. Tendency of the helicopter to drift laterally.

vertical fin, or vertical stabilizer. Located at the rear most portion of the helicopter (often referred to as the tail).

Chapter 1
Ground Operations

Preflight Inspection

Purpose

The pilot is the final authority in determining the airworthiness of the helicopter. This can be accomplished by conducting a visual inspection of the aircraft and aircraft documents.

Description

Prior to a visual inspection, check the maintenance logs to ensure compliance with:
- Annual inspections (once every 12 calendar months)
- Pitot-static/transponder Inspections (once every 24 calendar months)
- Airworthiness directives
- 100-hour inspections (if required)
- Oil changes (if required)
- Minimum equipment lists (MEL) (if associated with the helicopter)

After inspecting the maintenance records, proceed to the aircraft and ensure that the required paperwork is on board prior to flight. The acronym **ARROW** is a great tool to help you remember what is required:

Airworthiness Certificate

Registration Certificate

Radio Station License (required when flying outside the US)

Operating Handbook—Pilot's Operating Handbook (POH) or Rotorcraft Flight Manual (RFM)

Weight and Balance—This includes an equipment list specific to the helicopter

Now is a good time to check the fuel level so additional fuel can be ordered if necessary. After filling the tank, allow time for the fuel to settle and any contaminants that might be present to sink to the bottom before checking the fuel quality.

❶ Main Rotor Transmission Access

Cowl doors	Open
Static source	Check
Master switch	On
Warning lights	Check
Fuel gauge	Check quantity
Master switch	Off
Fuel quantity/cap	Confirm and secure
M/R transmission bolts and mounts	Secure, check for slippage
M/R trans: oil level, Telatemp	Check
M/R trans: chip detector	Wiring and safety
Upper frame assembly	Check for bends, cracks; secure
T/R push-pull tube	Check condition, secure; check travel, play
Forward flex coupling	Check bolts for slippage, cracks
Middle flex coupling	Check bolts for slippage, cracks
Clutch actuator bearing and Telatemp	Check condition
T/R bell crank	Secure; check travel, play
V-belts and pulley	Check condition
Wiring harness	Check condition and secure
Sheet metal structures	Inspect rivets; check for wrinkles and cracks
Cowl door	Closed

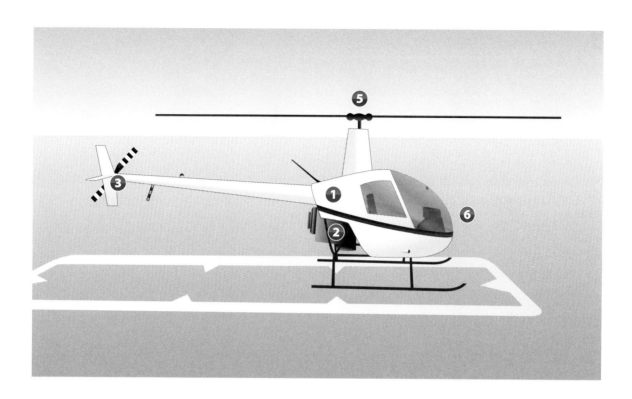

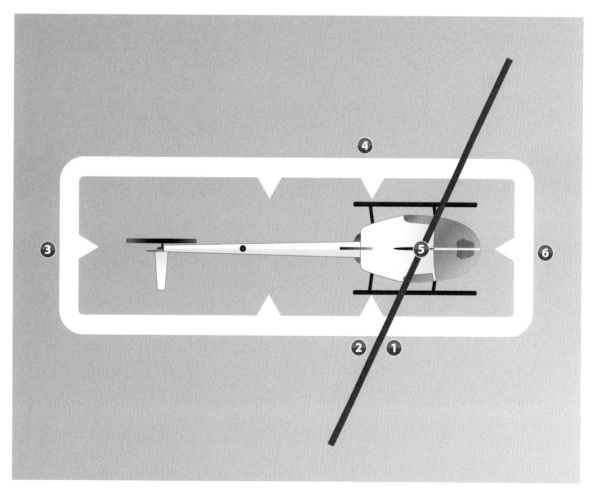

❷ Engine Area—Right Side

Left magneto	Check condition and secure
Starter relay	Secure, insulators
Lower frame assembly	Bends, cracks, secure
Engine (general)	Leaks, cracks, secure
Oil cooler and lines	Check condition and secure
Oil cooler access	Clear
Starter, ring gear	Check condition, secure
Lower sheave bearing, Telatemp	Check condition
Fan and scroll	Check condition, secure

❸ Tail Cone/Rotor

Attaching points	Bolts, cracks, slippage
Antenna, strobe	Check condition, secure
Tail cone (right side)	Check condition, rivets
Strobe light	Check condition, secure
Stabilizers, stinger	Check condition, cracks, secure
T/R gear box oil level	Check condition, safeties, secure
Anti-collision light	Check condition, secure
T/R gear box chip detector	Wiring, secure
T/R bell crank	Check condition, travel, secure
T/R P/C links	Check condition, play, secure
T/R Telatemp	Check
T/R blades	Check condition, secure, weights
Tail cone (left side)	Check condition, rivets
Tail cone attaching points	Bolts, cracks, slippage
Clutch actuator and wiring harness	Check condition, secure

❹ Engine Area—Left Side

Lower sheave, V-belts, ring gear, Telatemp	Check condition
Alternator, belt and hose	Check condition and secure
Engine (general)	Leaks, cracks, secure
Engine oil	5–6 quarts
Right magneto	Check condition, secure
Fuel line and gascolator	Check condition, secure
Throttle carburetor linkage	Secure, leaks
Lower frame assembly	Bends, cracks, secure

❺ Main Rotor

Pitch change links	Check play, safety wires
M/R seals, grips and root	Check condition, cracks, secure
M/R blades	Check condition, lamination, clean, level
Hub and hinge bolts	Check condition, cracks, bolt slippage
Boot and swash plates	Secure, check condition, play
M/R push-pull tube	Check condition, play

M/R blades	Turned to 3 and 9 o'clock positions
Mast cowling	Check condition, secure
Pitot tube	Positioned straight, forward, unobstructed
Fuel tank cap	Check quantity, secure
M/R tip/blade	Weights secure, blade condition

6 Cabin

Left skid gear, shoes and X-tubes	Check condition, secure
Navigation light	Secure, check condition
Fuselage and door (left)	Check condition, rivets, cotter pin
Bubble and trim string	Check condition, cracks, clean
Vent and landing lights	Unobstructed, clean, working
Lower fuselage and antenna	Check condition, rivets, cracks
Right skid gear, shoes and X-tubes	Check condition, secure
Navigation light	Secure, check condition
Fuselage and door (right)	Check condition, rivets, cotter pin
Hobbs time	Check
Required documents	Remember "ARROW" acronym
Fire extinguisher	Check
Auxiliary fuel tank sump	Drain
Main fuel tank sump	Drain
Gascolator	Drain

Common Errors

- Rushing the preflight in anticipation of flight.
- Not asking questions because you're afraid of looking ignorant.
- Merely going through the motions instead of doing a thorough check.

Tips

The preflight inspection is *very important*, so take your time! Always ask a mechanic if you're unsure about anything you find. Pilots will learn a lot about the systems of the helicopter when inspecting the aircraft prior to flight. If the preflight begins to feel routine, try doing it in reverse order. This will slow you down and help ensure that you're thoroughly checking everything on the list. Another way to vary the routine is to start in the middle of the list and complete it from a different starting point.

Private and Commercial PTS

Objective: To determine that the applicant—

1. Exhibits knowledge of the elements related to preflight inspection. This includes recognizing which items must be inspected, the reasons for checking each item, and how to detect possible defects.
2. Inspects the helicopter with reference to an appropriate checklist.
3. Verifies the helicopter is in condition for safe flight.

Engine Starting and Rotor Engagement

Purpose

This task is used to start the helicopter and engage the rotor system safely.

Description

Each helicopter has its own unique starting sequence depending on the make and model. In addition, operators may change the sequence of items in the POH checklist. This guide covers the engine starting procedure for the Robinson R22 helicopter and assumes that all preflight and before-starting checklists have been covered.

As a good rule of thumb, the helicopter should be placed on flat, level ground away from all obstructions and loose debris. Be sure that sufficient clearance is available around the helicopter to safely hover to your area of operations.

It is very important that you follow the factory recommended checklist for your specific aircraft. Some operators will adapt their own checklists to help with pilot "flow"; however, as the pilot-in-command (PIC) it is your responsibility to ensure that all items in the POH are covered.

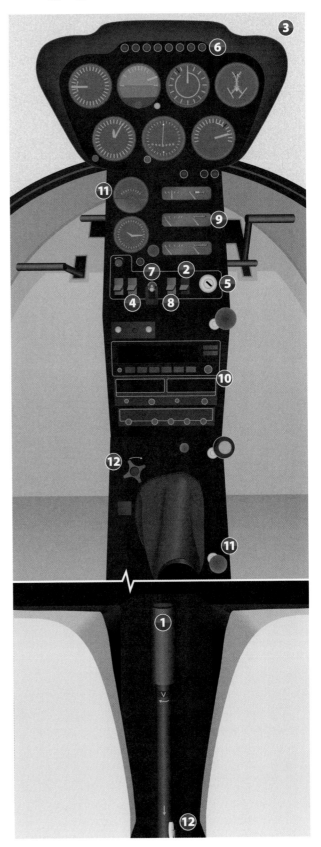

❶	Throttle twists for priming	As required
❶	Throttle	Closed
❷	Master switch	On
❸	Surrounding area	Clear
❹	Strobe light	On
❺	Ignition switch	To START position, then both
❻	Starter-on light	Out
❻	Set engine RPM	50–60%
❼	Clutch switch Blades turning	Engage Less than 5 seconds
❽	Alternator switch	On
❾	Oil Pressure within 30 seconds	25 psi minimum
❿	Avionics, headsets	On
❻	Clutch Light	Off
❻	Engine RPM	70–75%
❾	Engine gauges	Green
❺	Magnetos drop at 75%	Max 7% in 2 seconds
⓫	Carb heat check	Carb air temp. (CAT) gauge rise/drop
❶	Sprag clutch check from 75% RPM Doors Limit MAP (manifold air pressure) chart	Needles split Closed and latched Check
⓬	Cyclic and collective frictions	Off
❶	Governor on, increase throttle	RPM 102–104%
❻	Warning lights	Out
❶	Lift collective slightly, reduce RPM	Horn/light at 97%

⚠ **CAUTION:** Avoid continuous operation at rotor speed of 60–70% to minimize tail resonance.
On slippery surfaces, be prepared to counter nose-right rotation with left pedal as governor increases RPM.

Note: During run-up and shutdown, uncover your right ear, open right door, and listen for unusual bearing noise. Failing bearings will produce an audible whine or growl well before final failure.

Common Errors

- Failure to keep throttle closed during engine start-up.
- Not clearing the area of people or hazards.
- Turning the engine off when checking the magnetos.
- Rushing through the checklists.
- Not using checklists and performing the tasks from memory.

Tips

Make absolutely sure the throttle is closed when starting the engine. If it is not, the engine will quickly overspeed with no rotor system engaged to slow the rate of acceleration. If the engine rapidly increases on initial start up, damage to the fan scroll could result, which will require it to be balanced or replaced. If the key is inadvertently turned to the OFF position during magneto check, *do not* turn it back on. Quickly turning the key back to the BOTH position may damage the gears in the magnetos. Instead, allow the clutch to disengage and the rotors to stop turning before attempting a re-start. Go back to the beginning of the checklist and start again.

Private PTS

Objective: To determine that the applicant—

1. Exhibits knowledge of the elements related to correct engine starting procedures. This includes the use of an external power source and starting under various atmospheric conditions.

2. Positions the helicopter properly considering structures, surface conditions, other aircraft, and the safety of nearby persons and property.

3. Uses the appropriate checklist for starting procedure.

Commercial PTS

Objective: To determine that the applicant—

1. Exhibits knowledge of the elements related to correct engine starting procedures. This includes the use of an external power source, starting under various atmospheric conditions, awareness of other persons and property during start, and the effects of using incorrect starting procedures.

2. Ensures proper rotor blade clearance and friction flight controls, as necessary.

3. Uses the appropriate checklist for starting procedures.

Before Takeoff Check

Purpose

The before takeoff check is used to safely prepare the helicopter for flight.

Description

Follow all checklists to safely prepare the helicopter. The checked items should include performance limitations, caution/warning lights out, engine gauges in normal operating ranges, and visual inspection of the aircraft surroundings prior to lift off. Also check the power available for the day; most helicopters have a chart that is readable from the pilot's seat. Determine the Limit Manifold Pressure (LMP) and your Maximum Continuous Power (MCP) by referencing the chart. If the helicopter is turbine-powered, refer to the yellow arc and red line on both the torque and TOT (turbine outlet temperature) gauges.

The before takeoff check will vary from helicopter to helicopter; however, once the helicopter is ready to fly it is helpful to say out loud, "All caution and warning lights are out, rotor is 104%, engine gauges are in the green, and we have fuel." (Robinson R22 pilots add: "CAT gauge is out of the yellow.")

Once the helicopter is at flight idle with the collective fully down, be aware of your surroundings by performing a four-step clearing procedure.

1 Visually inspect the area around the helicopter to the right and say "Clear Right."

2 Visually inspect the area around the helicopter to the left and say "Clear Left."

3 Visually inspect the area in front of the helicopter and say "Clear Front."

4 Visually inspect the area above the helicopter and say "Clear Above."

Common Errors

- Rushing through the checklists.
- Not saying the visual checks out loud.
- Saying the visual checks out loud without really checking the gauges.

Tips

It is easy to overlook or rush this maneuver. Slow down and make sure to really inspect each item. It may be helpful to say out loud specific things like "Engine temperature is 305 degrees" or "Clear right, but there is a helicopter 30 yards away." Any slight variation from the normal checklist procedure is helpful in fighting complacency.

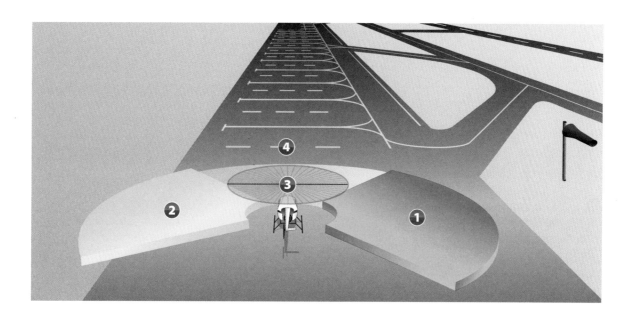

Private and Commercial PTS

Objective: To determine that the applicant—

1. Exhibits knowledge of the elements related to the before takeoff check. This includes the reasons for checking each item and how to detect malfunctions.
2. Positions the helicopter properly considering other aircraft, wind, and surface conditions.
3. Divides attention between inside and outside the cockpit.
4. Ensures that the engine temperature and pressure are suitable for run-up and takeoff.
5. Accomplishes the before takeoff check and ensures that the helicopter is in safe operating condition.
6. Reviews takeoff performance airspeeds, takeoff distances, departure, and emergency procedures.
7. Avoids runway incursions and/or ensures no conflict with traffic prior to takeoff.

Vertical Takeoff to a Hover

Purpose

The vertical takeoff to a hover is used to transition the helicopter from the ground to a stabilized 3–5 foot hover while remaining over a centered point.

Description

After completing a before takeoff check, visually clear the helicopter left, right, front, and overhead for obstructions.

1 Start with the collective full down and the cyclic and pedals in neutral position.

Slowly increase the collective. You will typically need to use a small amount of left pedal to compensate for the increased torque. As the helicopter becomes light on the skids, select a reference point 50 to 75 feet in front of the helicopter and neutralize all aircraft movement with the cyclic and pedals.

2 Continue to increase the collective smoothly and slowly, maintaining heading with slight pedal corrections.

As the helicopter becomes light on the skids, use extreme caution to avoid any rearward or lateral movement. If any lateral or rearward motion occurs, immediately lower the collective and begin again. The helicopter should rise vertically. Maintain heading with the pedals, maintain position over the ground with the cyclic, and maintain altitude with the collective. Once the helicopter is in a stabilized hover, perform a power check and verify that you are using the correct estimated power for that particular day.

After attaining a stabilized 3-foot hover, perform hover check:

1. RPM—104%
2. Engine instruments—green range
3. Hover power (manifold pressure)
4. Hover height—3 feet

Common Errors

- Failure to ascend vertically at a suitable rate.
- Failure to recognize and correct undesirable drift.
- Improper heading control.
- Overcontrol of cyclic, collective, or pedals.

Tips

In the case of a forward center of gravity (CG) configuration, the nose of the helicopter will remain on the ground as the tail/heels of the skids raise off the ground first. In the case of a rearward CG, the nose of the helicopter will rise off the ground first. Even lateral CG should be taken into consideration when lifting the helicopter to a hover; one side may lift off sooner than the other. Always keep in mind the potential for dynamic rollover.

Private and Commercial PTS

Objective: To determine that the applicant—

1. Exhibits knowledge of the elements related to a vertical takeoff to a hover and landing from a hover.
2. Ascends to and maintains recommended hovering altitude, and descends from recommended hovering altitude in headwind, crosswind, and tailwind conditions.
3. Maintains RPM within normal limits.
4. Establishes recommended hovering altitude, ±$\frac{1}{2}$ of that altitude within 10 feet of the surface; if above 10 feet, ±5 feet.

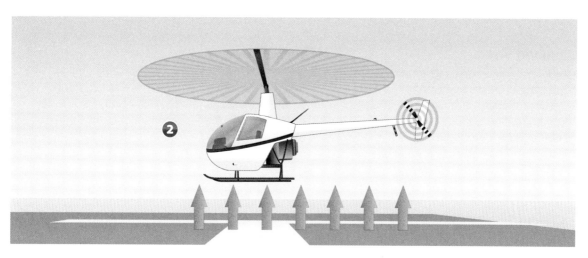

5. Avoids conditions that might lead to loss of tail rotor/antitorque effectiveness.

6. Maintains position within 4 feet (for private) or 2 feet (for commercial) of a designated point, with no aft movement.

7. Descends vertically to within 4 feet (for private) or 2 feet (for commercial) of the designated touchdown point.

8. Maintains specified heading, ±10°.

Surface Taxi

Purpose

This maneuver is used when the helicopter is unable to maintain a hover due to inadequate power. Surface taxiing is the intentional movement of the helicopter, under its own power, while the skids remain in contact with the ground surface. If the helicopter is equipped with wheels, the same technique is used in the application of controls. Regardless of the type of landing gear, this maneuver should only be performed on *smooth level surfaces*.

Description

1 The maneuver starts from a stationary position on a smooth surface with the collective pitch full down and the cyclic in the neutral position.

2 Tilt the rotor disc forward by moving the cyclic forward of the neutral position and apply a gradual upward pressure on the collective until the helicopter begins to move forward along the surface.
  • The pedals maintain heading.
  • The cyclic maintains ground track.
  • The collective controls starting, stopping and rate of speed.

Surface taxi at a speed no greater than a slow walk. During crosswind taxi, hold the cyclic into the wind to eliminate any drifting movement.

Common Errors

• Failure to keep skids aligned with path of movement (beware of dynamic rollover).
• Failure to maintain runway/taxiway centerline between helicopter skids (sliding off to one side).
• Use of aft cyclic to slow down or control speed.

Tips

A skid-equipped helicopter may require an additional amount of forward cyclic to start the helicopter moving. However, as it accelerates, it is important to remove the additional forward cyclic in order to maintain unaccelerated taxiing speed.

Private and Commercial PTS:

Objective: To determine that the applicant—

1. Exhibits knowledge of the elements related to surface taxiing.
2. Surface taxies the helicopter from one point to another under headwind, crosswind, and tailwind conditions, with the landing gear in contact with the surface, avoiding conditions that might lead to loss of tail rotor/antitorque effectiveness.
3. Properly uses cyclic, collective, and brakes to control speed while taxiing.
4. Properly positions nosewheel/tailwheel (if applicable), locked or unlocked.
5. Maintains RPM within normal limits.
6. Maintains appropriate speed for existing conditions.
7. Stops helicopter within ±4 feet (for private) or ±2 feet (for commercial) of a specified point.
8. Maintains specified track within ±4 feet (for private) or ±2 feet (for commercial).

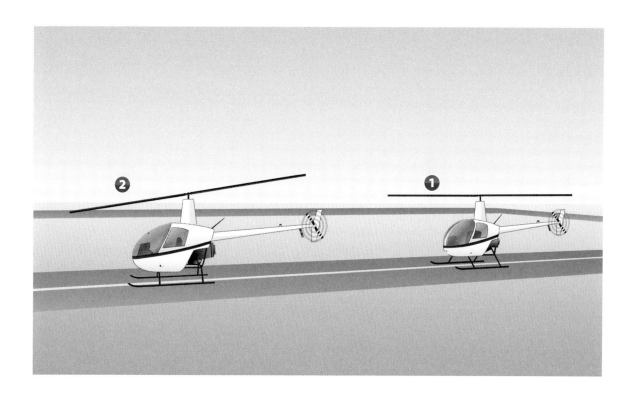

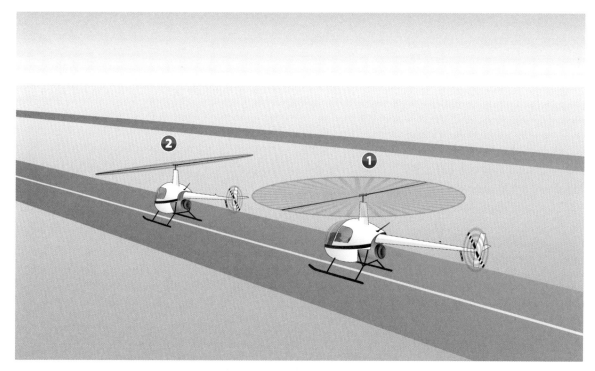

Hover Taxi

Purpose

The hover taxi is used to maneuver the helicopter from one location to another while hovering above the ground in a safe and stabilized manner.

Description

1 From a stabilized 3-foot hover, smoothly move the cyclic towards the direction of flight. Maintain altitude with the collective and heading with the pedals.

2 As movement begins, adjust the cyclic to keep the ground speed at a constant rate equivalent to a normal walk. Keep your eyes focused outside at least 50–75 feet along the intended flight path.
- The cyclic controls the flight path and speed.
- The collective controls height above ground.
- The pedals control heading.

To stop the movement, apply cyclic opposite of the direction of movement until the helicopter stops. During all phases of hovering, cyclic changes should be small and smooth to minimize the effects of overcontrolling or pendular action.

A hover taxi should always be completed with the skids aligned with the intended path. Never crab into the wind. The cyclic must be inclined into the wind enough to cancel out any tendency for the helicopter to drift.

Common Errors

- Improper control of heading and track.
- Erratic altitude control.
- Misuse of flight controls.
- Overcontrolling tendencies or "stirring the pot" cyclic inputs.

Tips

Keep your eyes focused outside at least 50–75 feet in front of the helicopter. It's almost impossible to hover the helicopter completely perfectly. Fix any mistakes as you go and use small controlled inputs.

Private and Commercial PTS

Objective: To determine that the applicant—

1. Exhibits knowledge of the elements related to hover taxiing.
2. Hover taxies over specified ground references, demonstrating forward, sideward, and rearward hovering and hovering turns.
3. Maintains RPM within normal limits.
4. Maintains specified ground track within ±4 feet of a designated reference (for private) or within ±2 feet (for commercial) on straight legs.
5. Maintains constant rate of turn at pivot points.
6. Maintains position within ±4 feet (for private) or ±2 feet (for commercial) of each pivot point during turns.
7. *Private:* Makes a 360° pivoting turn, left and right, stopping within 10° of a specified heading.
   Commercial: Makes 90°, 180°, and 360° pivoting turns, stopping within 10° of specified headings.
8. Maintains recommended hovering altitude, ±½ of that altitude within 10 feet of the surface, if above 10 feet, ±5 feet.

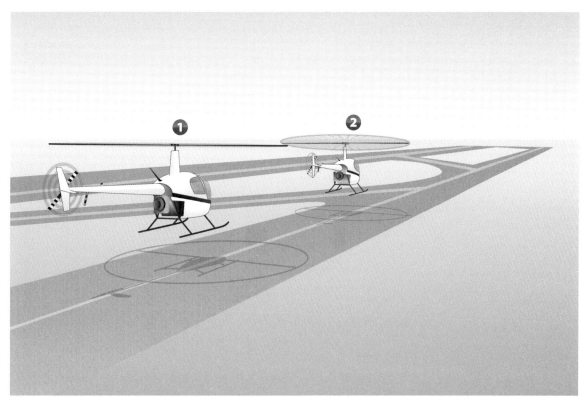

Hovering Exercises

Purpose

Hovering exercises are used to practice coordination of the flight controls through planned hovering maneuvers.

Description

Learning to hover the helicopter is one of the hardest maneuvers to master. The coordination required is tough for anyone, but these simple exercises can help you along the way.

1 The box pattern

Predetermine a box on the surface of a taxiway or infield grass and clear the area of any obstacles. Performing this maneuver on any active runway is not recommended, as your attention may be diverted from local traffic. Begin this maneuver in a corner of your box heading into the wind. From a stabilized 3-foot hover, apply cyclic in the direction of travel to follow the box pattern, and maintain heading with the pedals and altitude with the collective. Keep your eyes focused outside, at least 50 feet in front of the helicopter and use your peripheral vision to obtain your visual cues. This maneuver is easiest when heading into the wind. Once mastered, vary the direction to a crosswind or a tailwind to increase the difficulty.

2 Nose around a point

Pick a point on the ground and visualize a circle approximately 10 feet away from the predetermined point in the center. Be sure to clear the area of any obstacles. From a stabilized 3-foot hover, apply lateral cyclic along the visualized circle. Use the collective to maintain height and use the pedals to maintain heading. Keep your nose on the point as you hover around, and maintain a 10-foot distance from the center point. As the helicopter travels around in a circle, be mindful of the wind. Hold additional cyclic into the wind as necessary to maintain a constant distance. Try it clockwise first, then reverse course and try the maneuver counterclockwise. In high-wind situations keep a higher-than-normal hover height to ensure all parts of the helicopter maintain clearance from the ground.

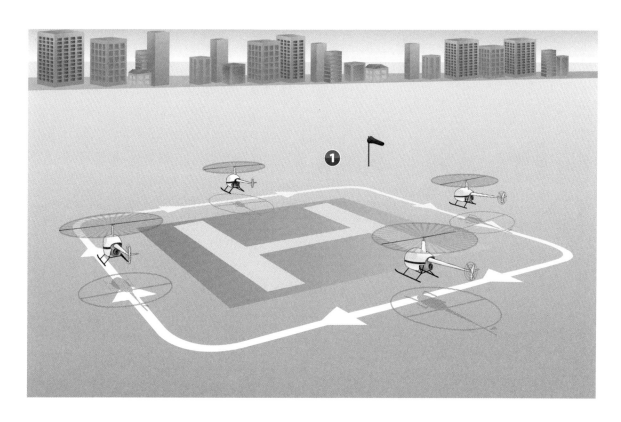

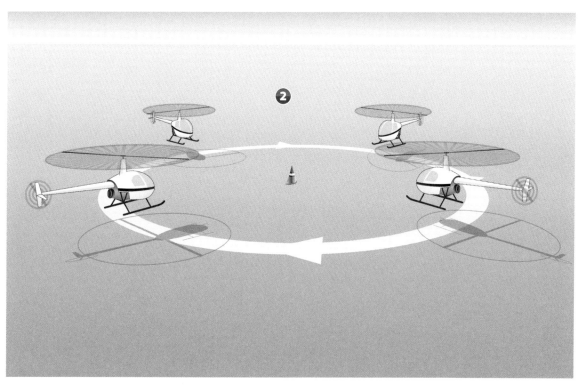

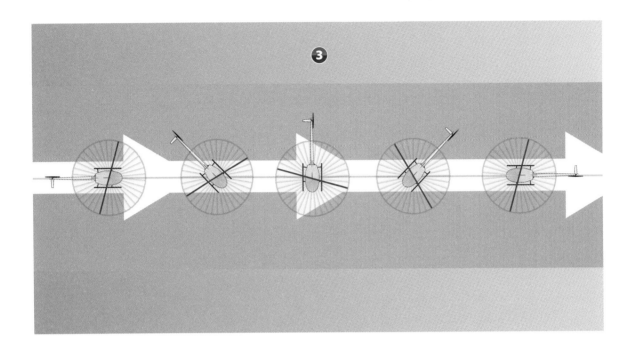

❸ Turning about the rotor mast axis

While hovering down the taxiway at the speed of a constant, fast-paced walk, apply the pedal to obtain a constant-rate turn. (A rate of 360° in 15–30 seconds is recommended.) Once a full revolution is completed, apply the opposite pedal to stop the turn and start turning in the opposite direction. Use the cyclic to control your path and rate of movement over the ground. Use the collective to control altitude above the ground and use the pedals to control the rate of turn. This is an advanced practice maneuver, and care should be taken at all times to avoid coming in contact with the surface, obstacles or other aircraft. An easy way to transition into this maneuver is to begin by performing only 90-degree turns while maintaining a constant speed over the ground. Once the flight controls are coordinated, move on to practice constant turning about the main rotor axis.

Common Errors

- Improper control of heading and track.
- Erratic altitude control.
- Misuse of flight controls.
- Overcontrolling tendencies or "stirring the pot" cyclic inputs.

Tips

Wind plays a huge factor in coordinated hovering. The strength of wind will determine the amount of required cyclic.

Be aware of your surroundings at all times. It is easy for pilots to be so focused on performing a maneuver that they lose sight of obstructions in their intended path.

Be gentle on all controls as it is easy to overcontrol the helicopter (provide too much of a corrective control input).

Private and Commercial PTS:

The PTS do not apply in this case, as these are exercises for pilot proficiency.

Vertical Landing from a Hover

Purpose

The vertical landing from a hover is used to transition the helicopter from a stabilized hover to the surface.

Description

1 From a stabilized 3-foot hover headed into the wind, lower the collective slightly to establish a slow rate of sink. Use a small amount of right pedal to maintain heading. Direct your vision 50 – 70 feet in front of the helicopter. Do not look immediately in front of the helicopter as this will lead to overcontrolling.

2 As the helicopter descends to about 6 inches above the ground, additional downward pressure on the collective may be necessary to overcome the increase in ground effect. As the skids make ground contact, neutralize all aircraft movement with cyclic and pedals. Continue to lower the collective smoothly until it is full down. Due to the nose-low attitude of the R22 with two people aboard, the toes of the skids will normally touch first on level terrain. A slight amount of forward and left cyclic will be necessary as ground contact is made. During solo flight, the attitude of the R22 is nose high and may require aft and right cyclic when ground contact is made.

Common Errors

- Failure to descend at a controlled rate.
- Rapidly lowering the collective at the first touch of the skid to the ground.
- Failure to recognize and correct undesirable drift.
- Improper heading control with the pedals.
- Overcontrol of cyclic, collective, and pedals.

Tips

The helicopter's CG location might prevent both skids from contacting the ground evenly or simultaneously. The toe(s) or heel(s) of one or both skids may touch the ground first. Also, lateral CG should be taken into consideration, as the helicopter may be right-skid or left-skid heavy. In a forward, left-skid-heavy situation the left toe of the skid will touch down first, followed by the left heel, then right skid. It is important to keep flying the helicopter until all parts of the skids are on the ground. Treat every landing as a slope landing and never rapidly lower the collective on the first contact with the ground. Always keep in mind the potential for dynamic rollover.

Private and Commercial PTS

Objective: To determine that the applicant—

1. Exhibits knowledge of the elements related to a vertical takeoff to a hover and landing from a hover.
2. Ascends to and maintains recommended hovering altitude and descends from recommended hovering altitude in headwind, crosswind, and tailwind conditions.
3. Maintains RPM within normal limits.
4. Establishes recommended hovering altitude, $\pm\frac{1}{2}$ of that altitude within 10 feet of the surface; if above 10 feet, ±5 feet.
5. Avoids conditions that might lead to loss of tail rotor/antitorque effectiveness.
6. Maintains position within 4 feet (for private) or 2 feet (for commercial) of a designated point, with no aft movement.
7. Descends vertically to within 4 feet (for private) or 2 feet (for commercial) of the designated touchdown point.
8. Maintains specified heading, ±10°.

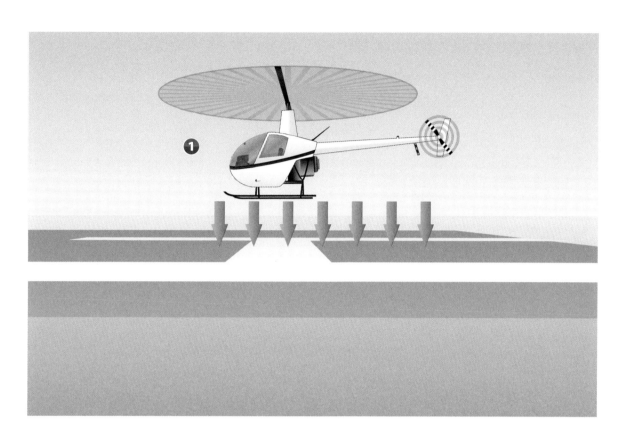

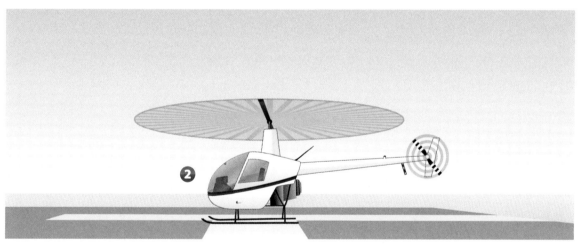

Post-Flight Procedures

Purpose

The purpose of the post-flight check is to safely shutdown the helicopter and conduct the post-flight inspection.

Description

Many pilots overlook the importance of a post-flight inspection because they are more focused on safely flying the helicopter. During the post-flight inspection, pilots should inspect the helicopter in order to determine whether any damage has occurred and what maintenance actions are required before the aircraft is flown again. The post-flight inspection checklist will vary depending on the helicopter and the operator's normal procedures. Some operators will adapt their own checklists to help with task "flow." However, as pilot in command it is your responsibility to ensure that all items in the POH are covered. Once the helicopter has landed, use the following checklist as a reference. (This checklist is geared towards Robinson R22 pilots.)

1	Collective	Full down
1	Engine RPM	75%
1	Governor	Off
2	Collective friction	On
2	Cyclic and pedals neutral Start Timer	Friction on 100-second cool down
3	Navigation and landing lights	Off
1	After 100 seconds	Throttle to idle
4	Cylinder head temperature	CHT drop, maximum 300°
5	Clutch Wait	Disengaged 30 seconds
6	Mixture	Idle cut off
7	Magnetos	Off
8	Alternator	Off
9	Radios/transponder Wait 30 seconds	Off Apply Rotor Brake
10	Clutch light	Off
11	Strobe and master switch	Off
12	Post-flight walk-around	Check overall general condition

During the post-flight walk-around, look for any fluid leaking, and any new dents and/or scratches that may have occurred. Specific operator procedures may require that the blades be placed in the 12/6 o'clock position (in a two-bladed system) or slightly off to one side (11/5 o'clock position) due to high-wind blade flapping while on the ground. In three- or four-bladed rotor systems, follow factory recommendations for static blade securing procedures.

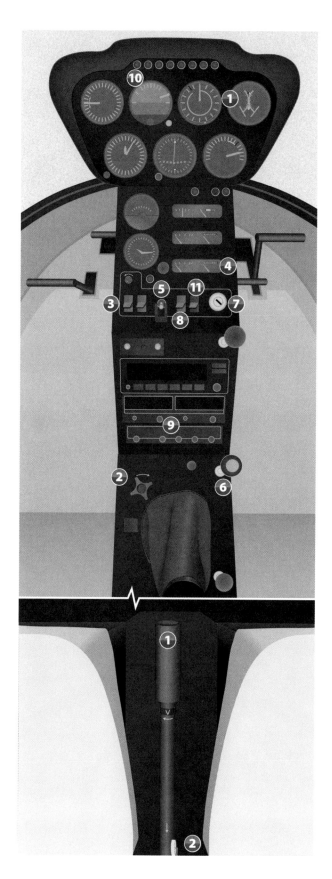

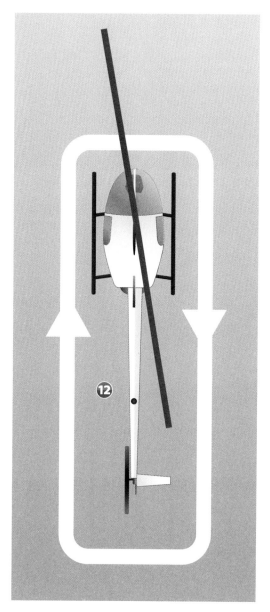

Common Errors

- Rushing the post-flight inspection.
- Forgetting to pull the mixture once the clutch is disengaged.
- Getting distracted.
- Not performing the post-flight inspection walk-around.

Tips

The post-flight inspection is an important part of the flight and is often overlooked. Keep your guard up for anything unusual during the walk-around, and try doing your normal preflight inspection backwards to change things up.

Private and Commercial PTS:

Objective: To determine that the applicant—

1. Exhibits knowledge of the elements related to after-landing, parking and securing procedures
2. Minimizes the hazardous effects of rotor downwash during hovering.
3. Parks in an appropriate area, considering the safety of nearby persons and property.
4. Follows the appropriate procedure for engine shutdown.
5. Completes the appropriate checklist.
6. Conducts an appropriate post-flight inspection and secures the aircraft.

Chapter 2
Basic Maneuvers

Straight-and-Level Flight

Purpose

Straight-and-level flight is achieved by maintaining constant airspeed, altitude, and heading.

Description

1 Level flight attitude

A level flight attitude is best determined by referencing the horizon with a fixed point in the cockpit, such as the magnetic compass or the tip path plane. Attitude or pitch control with the cyclic is the most important aspect of straight-and-level flight. The pilot will be able to detect changes in attitude by noting changes between the fixed point and the horizon.

Airspeed in cruise flight is determined by attitude and controlled by the cyclic. The cyclic control is very sensitive and requires very slight pressure to effect a change. Normal cruise airspeed for training is 70 KIAS. Primarily, the collective controls altitude. Cruise power (manifold pressure in the Robinson R22) is controlled by the collective, and the manifold pressure setting at 70 KIAS maintains a level flight altitude.

Each collective movement will require a corresponding pedal adjustment to maintain the aircraft in trim. An increase of collective will require additional left pedal to counter the increase in torque. Conversely, a collective decrease will require additional right pedal. Additionally, when the collective is increased, the nose will tend to rise, requiring slight forward cyclic to maintain a level or cruise flight attitude. The opposite is true with a decrease in collective pitch; the nose will move down, requiring a slight aft cyclic.

Common Errors

- Improper coordination of flight controls.
- Overcontrolling the cyclic.
- Failure to cross-check and correctly interpret outside and instrument references.
- Faulty trim technique.
- Fixation on instruments.

Tips

Straight-and-level flight is hard to master early on. Because of altitude, pilots may not immediately notice a nose-low (accelerating) or a nose-high (decelerating) attitude. Try stabilizing the attitude of the helicopter using a reference inside the cockpit, such as the compass mounting bolts. Keep in mind that once an input has been made with the cyclic, it may take a second to see the change in the helicopter's attitude. This can lead to overcontrolling of the cyclic, so try resting your right arm on your right leg to minimize hand movements.

Private and Commercial PTS

Straight-and-level flight is not a separate PTS task—it is done in the context of other PTS tasks; therefore there are no specific standards to reference for it. Instead you can use the standards for traffic pattern operations:

- Maintains traffic pattern altitude ±100 feet, and appropriate airspeed, ±10 knots.

View from inside cockpit

Normal Climbs

Purpose

The normal climb maneuver is used to practice a climb in altitude at a controlled rate.

Description

1 Clear the airspace around the aircraft by visually scanning for traffic. Note the manifold pressure necessary to maintain a 70 KIAS attitude.

2 Initiate the climb by raising the collective to increase manifold pressure 2–3" above cruise power, and establish a 500 feet per minute climb. Add a slight amount of aft cyclic pressure to slow the aircraft into a 60 KIAS attitude. Maintain aircraft trim with a slight amount of left pedal due to the increase in collective.

3 Fifty feet prior to reaching the desired altitude, begin to level off by applying forward cyclic and lowering the nose to a 70 KIAS attitude.

4 Once the helicopter has accelerated to 70 KIAS, slowly decrease the collective to cruise power (manifold pressure setting for level flight at 70 KIAS). A small amount of right pedal may be needed to trim the aircraft due to the decrease in collective.

Throughout the climb and level-off, continually cross-check outside references (attitude and heading) with inside references (flight instruments).

Common Errors

- Too much cyclic input.
- Airspeed too slow/fast.
- Overshooting or undershooting desired altitude.
- Trim not properly maintained.

Tips

Try using the 10% rule for leveling off. For example if you are climbing at 500 feet per minute, initiate the level-off procedure 50 feet prior to your desired altitude.

Private and Commercial PTS

A normal climb is not a separate PTS task—it is done in the context of other PTS tasks; therefore there are no specific standards to reference for it. For practice purposes, try maintaining the standards for normal/crosswind takeoffs and climbs:
- Recommended climb airspeed ±10 KIAS (for private) or ±5 KIAS (for commercial).
- Maintain RPM within normal limits.
- Maintain proper ground track with crosswind correction, if necessary.
- Remain aware of the possibility of wind shear and/or wake turbulence.

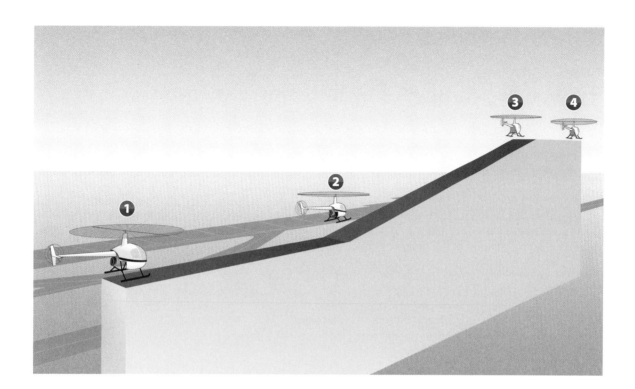

Normal Descents

Purpose

The normal descent maneuver is used to descend in altitude at a controlled rate.

Description

1 Clear the airspace around the aircraft by visually scanning for traffic. Note the manifold pressure necessary to maintain a 70 KIAS attitude.

2 Initiate the descent: decrease manifold pressure to 4–5" below the cruise power setting by lowering the collective, which will provide about 500 feet per minute descent. Lowering the collective will reduce torque, requiring a slight amount of right pedal to maintain aircraft trim. Apply slight aft cyclic to adjust the attitude of the helicopter to 60 KIAS.

3 Fifty feet prior to reaching the desired altitude, begin to level off by slowly raising the collective to increase manifold pressure to 1" above cruise power. Maintain aircraft trim with left pedal.

4 Add a small amount of forward cyclic to re-establish a 70 KIAS cruise speed. Once the helicopter accelerates to 70 KIAS, lower the collective back to cruise power.

Common Errors

- Using cyclic inputs that are too large and or aggressive.
- Airspeed too slow/fast.
- Overshooting or undershooting desired altitude.
- Not properly maintaining trim.

Tips

Try using the 10% rule for leveling off. For example, if you are climbing at 500 feet per minute, initiate the level-off procedure 50 feet prior to your desired altitude.

Private and Commercial PTS

A normal descent is not a separate PTS task—it is done in the context of other PTS tasks; therefore there are no specific standards to reference for it. For practice purposes, try maintaining the standards for the normal/crosswind approach to a hover:

- Establish and maintain the normal approach angle, and proper rate of closure.
- Remain aware of the possibility of wind shear and/or wake turbulence.
- Avoid situations that may result in settling-with-power.
- Maintain proper ground track with crosswind correction, if necessary.
- Arrive at your determined altitude ±4 feet (for private) or ±2 feet (for commercial).

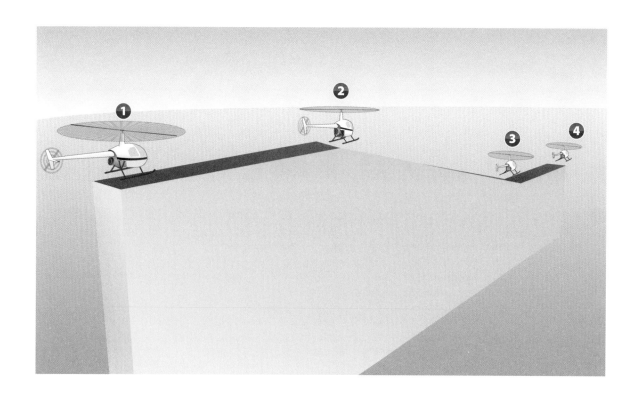

Level Turns

Purpose

The purpose of practicing level turns is to turn the aircraft using a constant angle of bank at a constant airspeed and altitude.

Description

1 From straight-and-level flight at 70 KIAS, clear the airspace around the aircraft and in the direction of the turn.

2 Smoothly apply the cyclic towards the direction of the turn until the desired angle of bank is reached. As the angle of bank increases, additional collective may be required to maintain altitude. If additional collective is added, apply the left pedal to maintain trim.

3 Use the horizon as a reference to maintain a 70 KIAS attitude and the desired angle of bank with the cyclic. Keep the aircraft in trim with the pedals.

4 Begin the recovery from the turn just prior to reaching the desired rollout heading. Apply the cyclic opposite the direction of the turn, and if any collective has been added during the turn, reduce it back to cruise power while maintaining the aircraft in trim with the pedals.

Common Errors

- Improper coordination of flight controls.
- Failure to cross-check and correctly interpret outside and instrument references.
- Faulty trim technique.
- Fixation on instruments.

Tips

Due to the pilot's arm position when manipulating the cyclic, new students will often rotate about their arm using their elbow as a pivot point.
To correct this:
- During left turns, add a small amount of forward cyclic.
- During right turns, add a small amount of aft cyclic.

Private and Commercial PTS

A level turn is not a separate PTS task—it is done in the context of other PTS tasks; therefore there are no specific standards to reference for it. For practice purposes, try maintaining the standards for traffic pattern operations:
- Correct for wind drift to maintain proper ground track.
- Maintain altitude ±100 feet.
- Maintain airspeed ±10 knots.

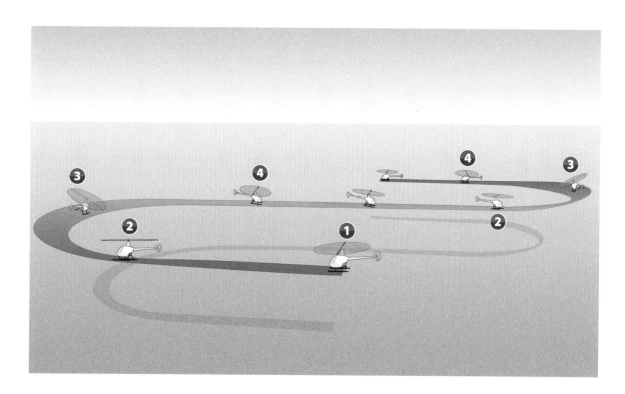

Acceleration

Purpose

The purpose of practicing acceleration is to learn to maintain a constant altitude and heading while accelerating the helicopter to a faster speed.

Description

Controlling the attitude of the helicopter is one of the most important tasks of a pilot. While maintaining a constant altitude, changing the attitude of the helicopter will change the requirements for power and subsequently the demand for antitorque.

From a 70 KIAS straight-and-level attitude, establish a reference point inside the helicopter that lines up with the horizon. (Robinson R22 pilots, try using the top of the compass or its attaching hardware as a reference point that lies on the horizon. This point will vary depending on the pilot's physical height.)

1 Clear the airspace in front of you, looking for any traffic that may be in the area. From straight-and-level flight at 70 KIAS, slowly raise the collective increasing manifold pressure approximately 2" above cruise power, adding left pedal to counteract torque, and forward cyclic to lower the nose of the helicopter, allowing your reference point to fall 2" below the horizon.

2 Allow a few seconds for the airspeed indicator to indicate an increase in airspeed. As the aircraft begins to accelerate, adjust cyclic, collective, and pedals as necessary to stabilize at 80 KIAS and level flight. Throughout the maneuver, maintain a constant cross-check of airspeed, altitude, trim and heading.

Common Errors

- Overcontrolling the cyclic.
- Flying out of trim.
- Abrupt control inputs.
- Failure to maintain altitude.

Tips

When adjusting attitude and airspeed, make small control inputs with the cyclic in order to avoid overcontrolling the helicopter.

Be patient waiting for the airspeed to change; there is a momentary delay between making a change in the cyclic and seeing the change on the airspeed indicator.

Private and Commercial PTS

Acceleration is not a separate PTS task—it is done in the context of other PTS tasks; therefore there are no specific standards to reference for it. For practice purposes try maintaining:
- Airspeed ±10 KIAS (for private) or ±5 KIAS (for commercial)
- Altitude ±100 feet (for private) or ±50 feet (for commercial)

View from inside cockpit

Deceleration

Purpose

The purpose of deceleration is to learn to maintain a constant altitude and heading while decelerating the helicopter to a slower speed.

Description

Controlling the attitude of the helicopter is one of the most important tasks of a pilot. While maintaining a constant altitude, changing the attitude of the helicopter will change the requirements for power and subsequently the demand for antitorque.

From a 70 KIAS straight-and-level attitude, establish a reference point inside the helicopter that lines up with the horizon. (Robinson R22 pilots, try using the top of the compass or its attaching hardware as a reference point that lies on the horizon. This point will vary depending on the pilot's physical height.)

1. Clear the airspace in front of you, looking for any traffic that may be in the area. From a straight-and-level flight at 70 KIAS, lower the collective decreasing manifold pressure by 2" from cruise power and apply corresponding right antitorque pedal. Add aft cyclic until your reference point is 2" above the horizon.

2. Allow a few seconds for the airspeed indicator to show a decrease in airspeed. As the aircraft begins to decelerate, adjust the cyclic, collective, and pedals as necessary to stabilize at 50 KIAS and level flight. Throughout the maneuver, maintain a constant cross-check of airspeed, altitude, trim and heading.

Common Errors

- Overcontrolling the cyclic.
- Flying out of trim.
- Abrupt control inputs.
- Failure to maintain altitude.

Tips

When adjusting attitude and airspeed, make small control inputs with the cyclic in order to avoid overcontrolling the helicopter.

Private and Commercial PTS

Deceleration is not a separate PTS task—it is done in the context of other PTS tasks; therefore there are no specific standards to reference for it. For practice purposes try maintaining:

- Airspeed ±10 KIAS (for private) or ±5 KIAS (for commercial).
- Altitude ±100 feet (for private) or ±50 feet (for commercial).

View from inside cockpit

Chapter 3
Airport Operations

Normal Takeoff from a Hover

Purpose

The purpose of practicing a normal takeoff from a hover is to transition the helicopter from a stabilized hover to a normal climb.

Description

Review the power-available chart for appropriate climb power. (Robinson R22 helicopters have an LMP and MCP.) Then clear the airspace of traffic with a 360-degree clearing turn and complete a before takeoff check. Check and say out loud the following items:

1. RPM normal (104% for R22s).
2. Warning lights out.
3. Engine instruments green.
4. Carb heat as required.
5. Hover power (Robinson R22, manifold pressure gauge).
6. 3- to 5-foot hover height.

Then you are ready to begin the maneuver.

1 From a stabilized 3-foot hover, select an object(s) along the takeoff path to use as a reference point for maintaining ground track. Begin the takeoff with a small amount of forward/left cyclic to get the helicopter moving forward. If the helicopter begins to settle, increase the collective to hold a 3-foot altitude and maintain heading with pedals.

2 As the airspeed increases to approximately 15 KIAS, effective translational lift (ETL) will occur. At ETL, lift will increase noticeably, causing the nose to pitch up. Apply sufficient forward/left cyclic to continue the acceleration. This will prevent the nose from rising. As you continue to accelerate, stay below 10' skid height to remain clear of the height-velocity diagram.

3 As the airspeed increases, the streamlining of the fuselage and the increased efficiency of the tail rotor will cause a left yaw, requiring a right pedal correction. Continue to smoothly accelerate, maintaining ground track to 50 KIAS of airspeed.

4 At an altitude of 8–10 feet and airspeed of 50 KIAS, apply a small amount of aft cyclic to rotate the helicopter into a climb while continuing to accelerate to 60 KIAS. If power is available, raise the collective to the appropriate takeoff power setting, being careful not to exceed approved limits. Continue climbing at 500 feet per minute or more using the climb power available.

5 Hold 60 KIAS when climbing and ascend to an altitude of at least 300 feet before turning crosswind.

Crosswind Considerations:

During crosswind takeoffs, the helicopter is flown in a slip to an altitude of 50 feet. To do this, place the cyclic into the wind as necessary to maintain the proper ground track. Apply the opposite pedal to align the fuselage with the ground track. Above 50 feet, crab the helicopter into the wind by putting the aircraft in trim with the pedals and maintaining ground track with cyclic.

Note: During the takeoff, the acceleration to climb speed and the appropriate altitude gain should be accomplished without entering the shaded areas of the height-velocity diagram.

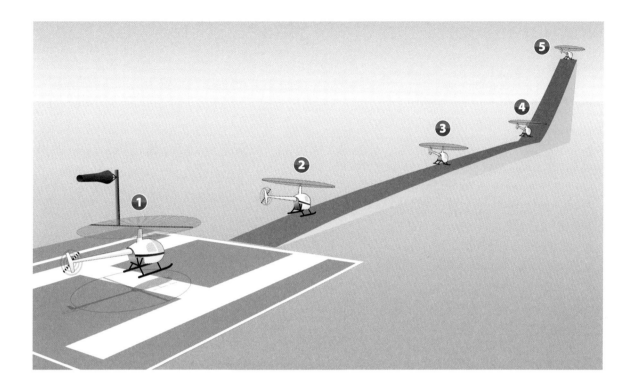

Common Errors

- Forgetting before takeoff checks.
- Applying too much forward cyclic from initial hover.
- Inability to control aircraft heading with pedal.
- Failure to anticipate the additional lift from ETL.
- Failure to keep desired ground track.
- Allowing the aircraft's nose to pitch up too much during the ETL transition.

Tips

On the initial acceleration, be careful not to apply too much forward cyclic or too much collective. Try using no more than the minimum power required to initiate the hover. A small amount of collective may be needed to keep your altitude above ground as you transition through ETL. Always be mindful of the height-velocity diagram to stay out of danger.

Private and Commercial PTS

Objective: To determine that the applicant—

1. Exhibits knowledge of the elements related to normal and crosswind takeoff and climb, including factors affecting performance, to include height/velocity information.
2. Establishes a stationary position on the surface or a stabilized hover prior to takeoff in headwind and crosswind conditions.
3. Maintains RPM within normal limits.
4. Accelerates to manufacturer's recommended climb airspeed, ±10 knots (for private) or ±5 knots (for commercial).
5. Maintains proper ground track with crosswind correction, as necessary.
6. Remains aware of the possibility of wind shear and/or wake turbulence.

Normal Takeoff from the Surface

Purpose

The purpose of a normal takeoff from the surface is to conduct a no-hover takeoff when loose snow or dusty conditions exist.

Description

Review the power-available chart for appropriate climb power. (Robinson R22 helicopters have an LMP and MCP.) Then complete a before takeoff check. Check and say out loud the following items:

1. RPM normal (104% for R22s).
2. Warning lights out.
3. Engine instruments green.
4. Carb heat as required.
5. Hover power (Robinson R22, manifold pressure gauge).
6. 3- to 5-foot hover height.

Then you are ready to begin the maneuver. If you have any questions as to the takeoff/climb/cruise power settings, consult your instructor.

1. As the collective is raised and the helicopter becomes light on the skids, adjust the cyclic and pedals as necessary to prevent any lateral or rearward surface movement. Continue to apply collective pitch and, as the helicopter breaks ground, use cyclic as necessary to assure forward movement as altitude is gained.

2. As the airspeed increases to approximately 15 KIAS, effective translational lift (ETL) will occur. At ETL, lift will increase noticeably, causing the nose to pitch up. Apply sufficient forward/left cyclic to continue the acceleration. This will prevent the nose from rising.

3. As airspeed increases, the streamlining of the fuselage and the increased efficiency of the tail rotor will cause a left yaw, requiring a right pedal correction. Continue to smoothly accelerate, maintaining ground track to 50 KIAS of airspeed.

4. At an altitude of 8–10 feet and airspeed of 50 KIAS, apply small amount of aft cyclic to rotate the helicopter into a climb while continuing to accelerate to 60 KIAS. Continue climbing at 500 feet per minute or more using the climb power available.

5. Hold 60 KIAS when climbing and ascend to an altitude of at least 300 feet before turning crosswind.

Crosswind Considerations

During crosswind takeoffs, the helicopter is flown in a slip to an altitude of 50 feet. To do this, place the cyclic into the wind as necessary to maintain the proper ground track. Apply opposite pedal to align the fuselage with the ground track. Above 50 feet, crab the helicopter into the wind by putting the aircraft in trim with the pedals and maintaining ground track with the cyclic.

Note: During the takeoff, the acceleration to climb speed and the appropriate altitude gain should be accomplished without entering the shaded areas of the height-velocity diagram.

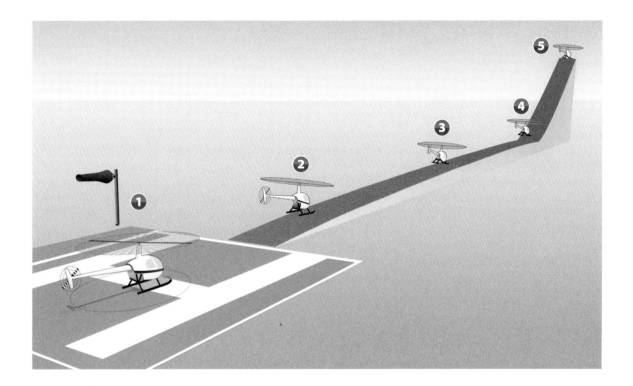

Common Errors

- Improper use of cyclic, collective, or pedals.
- Failure to maintain heading or ground track.
- Failure to attain effective translational lift prior to attempting transition to flight.
- Gaining excessive altitude prior to attaining climb airspeed.
- Failure to establish and maintain climb power and airspeed.

Tips

Keep in mind that the initial increase in power requires more antitorque pedal to compensate (Robinson R22s require more left pedal). Be sure to keep the nose of the helicopter aligned with the path of the helicopter. Always be mindful of the height-velocity diagram to stay out of danger.

Private and Commercial PTS

Objective: To determine that the applicant—

1. Exhibits knowledge of the elements related to normal and crosswind takeoff and climb, including factors affecting performance, to include height/velocity information.
2. Establishes a stationary position on the surface or a stabilized hover prior to takeoff in headwind and crosswind conditions.
3. Maintains RPM within normal limits.
4. Accelerates to manufacturer's recommended climb airspeed, ±10 knots (for private) or ±5 knots (for commercial).
5. Maintains proper ground track with crosswind correction, as necessary.
6. Remains aware of the possibility of wind shear and/or wake turbulence.

Traffic Pattern Operations

Purpose

For training purposes, traffic pattern operations are used to practice continual takeoffs and landings.

Description

A helicopter airport traffic pattern is similar to the airplane pattern, except it is at a lower altitude (500 AGL) and closer to the airport. This pattern should be on the opposite side of the runway (from the fixed-wing traffic), with turns in the opposite direction (unless local procedures dictate otherwise). When using the runways for traffic pattern operations, helicopter pilots will need more time than airplanes to decelerate and accelerate. Use the terminology "Stop and Go" rather than "Touch and Go" to announce your intentions. To further mitigate risk, use a taxiway or other suitable landing area whenever possible to minimize the possibility of runway incursions. When performing multiple traffic patterns it is important for pilots to make an effort to fly in a neighborly manner by following local noise-abatement procedures found in the Airport/Facilities Directory (A/FD).

When considering ground paths for the traffic pattern, be sure to fly over good forced-landing areas. If you can't, take steps to minimize the risks.

1 Upwind Leg

During takeoff, an effort should be made to stay outside the height-velocity diagram. Assume a normal climb at 60 KIAS. Upon reaching 300 feet, visually clear the airspace to the right and begin a 90° turn to crosswind, continuing a 60 KIAS climb. Set the collective to climb power (Robinson R22: manifold pressure) during climb.

2 Crosswind Leg

Maintain ground track by crabbing the helicopter into the wind. Fifty feet prior to reaching 500 feet AGL, clear the airspace to the right and begin a 90° right turn downwind while accelerating to 70 KIAS, then reduce power to cruise 70 KIAS.

3 Downwind Leg

Ground speed will increase due to the downwind condition. Fly the downwind leg at 70 KIAS and 500 feet AGL using ground reference points to maintain ground track. Perform a pre-landing check when abeam the landing site. Upon reaching a location 45° past the point of landing, decrease the collective to establish a descent, and maintain 70 KIAS. Once the descent is established, clear the airspace and turn to the right. Begin a 90° turn and place the aircraft in a 60 KIAS attitude by adding aft cyclic. This turn will require a steeper angle of bank due to the downwind condition.

4 Base Leg

On base, descend to 300 feet AGL and continue to slow to 60 KIAS. Plan the turn from base to final so as to rollout aligned with the point of intended touchdown.

5 Final

Fly the final approach leg at 60 KIAS and 300 feet AGL until you reach the appropriate approach angle. Maintain approach angle with the collective, rate of closure with the cyclic, and heading with the pedals.

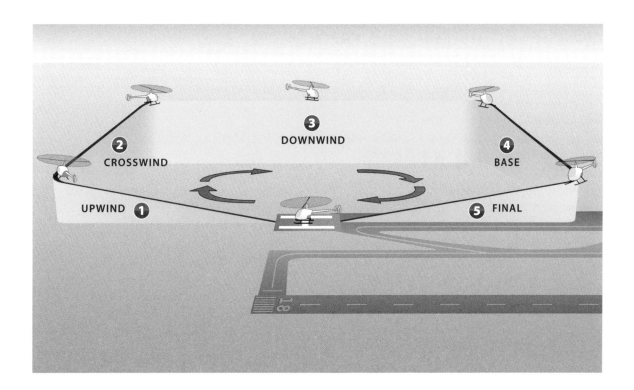

Common Errors

- Failure to comply with local traffic pattern instructions and procedures.
- Improper correction for wind drift.
- Inadequate spacing from traffic.
- Improper altitude or airspeed control.
- Overshooting the final approach angle.

Tips

At an uncontrolled airport you should make position reports during a turn because the helicopter's tilted rotor disc makes it more visible to other aircraft.

Private and Commercial PTS

Objective: To determine that the applicant—

1. Exhibits knowledge of the elements related to traffic patterns. This includes procedures at airports and heliports with and without operating control towers, prevention of runway incursions, collision avoidance, wake turbulence avoidance, and wind shear.
2. Complies with proper traffic pattern procedures.
3. Maintains proper spacing from other traffic and avoids the flow of fixed-wing aircraft.
4. Corrects for wind drift to maintain proper ground track.
5. Maintains orientation with runway/landing area in use.
6. Maintains traffic pattern altitude, ±100 feet, and the appropriate airspeed, ±10 knots.

Normal Approach to a Hover

Purpose

The normal approach to a hover is used to transition from flight at altitude to a stabilized 3–5 foot hover.

Description

On final approach, the helicopter should be headed into the wind, aligned with the point of intended touchdown, and at 60 KIAS and 300 feet AGL.

1 When a normal approach angle of 10–12 degrees is intercepted, begin the approach by lowering the collective sufficiently to establish descent at the proper approach angle. With the decrease in collective, the nose will tend to pitch down, requiring aft cyclic to maintain a 60 KIAS attitude and right pedal to maintain heading.

During the approach:
- Use the cyclic to control the rate of closure.
- Use the collective to control the rate of descent.
- Use the pedals to control the heading.

Maintain entry airspeed until the apparent ground speed and rate of closure appear to be increasing (should look like a brisk walk). Then add aft cyclic to slow the helicopter.

2 If a crosswind condition exists, crab into the wind above 50 feet. At approximately 25 to 40 feet, and dependent upon the wind, the helicopter will begin to lose effective translational lift. This loss will be felt as a lateral vibration and the aircraft will begin to settle. The pilot must anticipate the loss of ETL and compensate with increased collective to maintain the approach angle. The increase of collective will tend to make the nose rise, requiring forward cyclic to maintain proper rate of closure.

3 As the helicopter approaches an altitude of 3 feet, increase the collective to hold a 3-foot hover. Maintain aircraft heading with pedals. Slight aft cyclic input may be necessary to stop any forward movement.

Common Errors

- Improper use of cyclic to control rate of closure.
- Improper use of collective to control rate of descent.
- Failure to coordinate pedal corrections with power changes.
- Failure to arrive at termination point at zero ground speed.

Tips

The student can determine the proper approach angle by relating the point of intended touchdown to a point on the helicopter windshield. The collective controls the angle of approach.
- If the touchdown point seems to be moving up on the windshield, the angle is becoming shallower, necessitating a slight increase in collective.
- If the touchdown point moves down on the windshield, the approach angle is becoming steeper, requiring a slight decrease in collective.

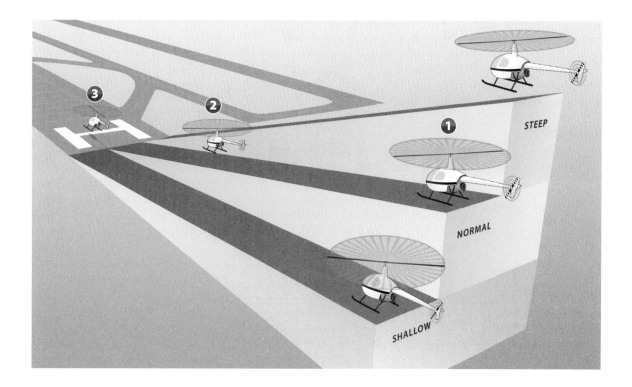

Private and Commercial PTS

Objective: To determine that the applicant—

1. Exhibits knowledge of the elements related to normal and crosswind approach.
2. Considers performance data, including height/velocity information.
3. Considers the wind conditions, landing surface, and obstacles.
4. Selects a suitable touchdown point (for private) or termination point (for commercial).
5. Establishes and maintains the normal approach angle and proper rate of closure.
6. Remains aware of the possibility of wind shear and/or wake turbulence.
7. Avoids situations that may result in settling-with-power.
8. Maintains proper ground track with crosswind correction, if necessary.
9. Arrives over the touchdown point (for private) or termination point (for commercial), on the surface or at a stabilized hover, ±4 feet (for private) or ±2 feet (for commercial).
10. Completes the prescribed checklist, if applicable.

Normal Approach to the Surface

Purpose

The purpose of the normal approach to the surface is to accomplish a normal approach when loose snow or dusty surface conditions exist.

Description

This technique will provide the most favorable visibility conditions and reduce the possibility of debris ingestion by the engine, main rotor and/or tail rotor.

This approach is initiated in the same manner as the normal or steep approach to a hover. However, instead of terminating at an altitude of 3 feet, the approach is continued until touchdown to the surface.

Touchdown should occur smoothly, with the skids level, ground speed zero, and a rate of descent approaching zero. Maintain the appropriate descent angle with the collective, heading with the pedals, and rate of closure with the cyclic.

Common Errors

- Improper use of cyclic to control rate of closure.
- Improper use of collective to control rate of descent.
- Failure to coordinate pedal corrections with power changes.
- Lateral movement upon touchdown.

Tips

Once inside ground effect, the pilot may need to further lower the collective for the helicopter to settle to the ground. Pilots should keep their eyes fixed on a point 50–75 feet in front of the helicopter and avoid focusing on any dust or snow particles that may be swirling about the aircraft.

Private and Commercial PTS

Objective: To determine that the applicant—

1. Exhibits knowledge of the elements related to normal and crosswind approach.
2. Considers performance data, including height/velocity information.
3. Considers the wind conditions, landing surface, and obstacles.
4. Selects a suitable touchdown point (for private) or termination point (for commercial).
5. Establishes and maintains the normal approach angle and proper rate of closure.
6. Remains aware of the possibility of wind shear and/or wake turbulence.
7. Avoids situations that may result in settling-with-power.
8. Maintains proper ground track with crosswind correction, if necessary.
9. Arrives over the touchdown point (for private) or termination point (for commercial), *on the surface* or at a stabilized hover, ±4 feet (for private) or ±2 feet (for commercial).
10. Completes the prescribed checklist, if applicable.

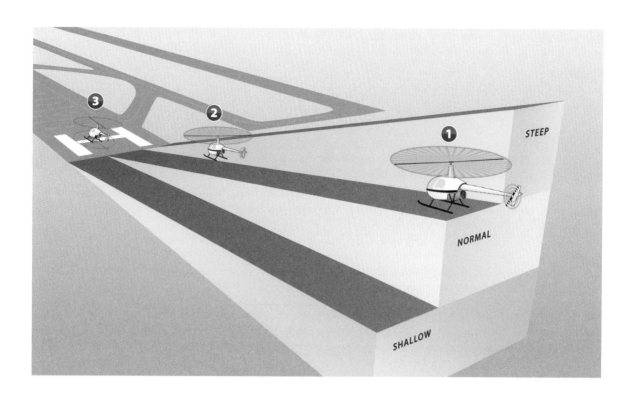

Go-Around Procedure

Purpose

The purpose of the go-around procedure is to abort an approach when the helicopter is in a position from which it is not safe to continue the approach.

Description

Any time a pilot feels an approach is uncomfortable, incorrect, or potentially dangerous, it should be abandoned. The decision to make a go-around should be initiated before a critical situation develops.

1 When the decision is made, carry it out without hesitation. When you initiate the go-around, increase the collective to takeoff power to stop the descent. Once the descent is stopped, add forward cyclic to accelerate the helicopter to 60 KIAS.

2 Upon reaching 60 KIAS, use gentle aft cyclic to initiate a climb. If aft cyclic is not introduced at 60 KIAS, the helicopter will continue to accelerate.

3 Climb to normal traffic pattern altitude for the upwind-to-crosswind turn. Keep in mind that it may be necessary to alter your course to avoid overflying other aircraft or if an unsafe condition exists on the ground. Always fly with the anticipation of an engine failure.

Common Errors

- Failure to recognize the need for a go-around.
- Hesitating to make the decision.
- Improper flight control applications during transition to climb.
- Failure to control drift and safely clear obstacles.

Tips

It is always preferable to go-around than to try to fix a problem on the way down. Helicopters are sometimes difficult to see, especially by high-winged aircraft that are on the ground. Keep an eye on ground traffic at all times to anticipate its location and movement.

Private and Commercial PTS

Objective: To determine that the applicant—

1. Exhibits knowledge of the elements related to a go-around and when it is necessary.
2. Makes a timely decision to discontinue the approach to landing.
3. Maintains RPM within normal limits.
4. Establishes proper control input to stop descent and initiate climb.
5. Retracts the landing gear, if applicable, after a positive rate-of-climb indication.
6. Maintains proper ground track with crosswind correction, if necessary.
7. Transitions to a normal climb airspeed, ±10 knots (for private) or ±5 knots (for commercial).
8. Completes the prescribed checklist, if applicable.

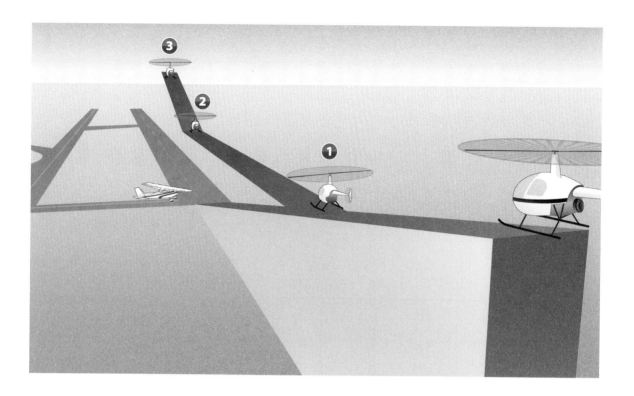

Chapter 4
Performance Operations

Maximum Performance Takeoff and Climb

Purpose

The purpose of practicing the maximum performance takeoff and climb is to simulate obstruction clearance and transition the helicopter from the surface to a maximum performance climb.

Description

While on the ground, check the manifold pressure limit chart to determine the maximum power available at the given pressure altitude and temperature. Clear the aircraft left, right and overhead, then complete a before takeoff check. Check and say out loud the following:

1. Rotor RPM 104%.
2. Warning lights out.
3. Engine instruments in the green.
4. We have fuel.
5. Carburetor heat out of the yellow.

Select reference point(s) along the takeoff path to maintain ground track.

1 Start the takeoff by slowly raising the collective until the helicopter becomes light on its skids. While light on the skids, pause for a moment to neutralize all movements of the helicopter. Slowly increase the collective and position the cyclic so as to break ground and maintain a 40 KIAS attitude (approximately the same attitude as when the helicopter is light on the skids). Continue to slowly increase the collective until you reach the maximum power available. This large collective movement will require a substantial increase in left pedal to maintain heading.

2 At 50 feet of altitude or when clear of obstacles, slowly lower the nose by adding forward cyclic to a normal 60 KIAS climb attitude.

3 As the airspeed passes 60 KIAS, reduce the collective to normal climb power (hover power manifold pressure).

This takeoff can also be accomplished starting from a 3-foot hover.

Common Errors

- Failure to resume normal climb power/ airspeed after passing over the obstacle.
- Once above ETL, failure to increase collective to resume maximum climb.
- Inability to stay within the limitations of the helicopter.
- Improper inputs to all 3 controls.
- Failure to do before takeoff check.

Tips

Don't rush the maneuver; there should be a balance between obtaining ETL and continuing to climb. Keep in mind that with the high power settings, the collective must be lowered immediately if there is an engine failure. If this happens, you should also alter your takeoff course to land as safely as possible.

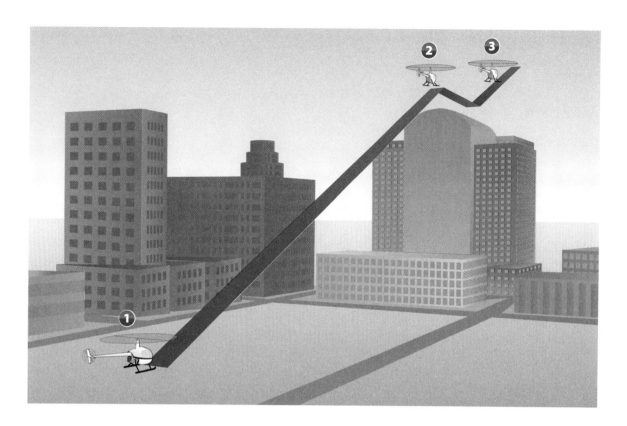

Private and Commercial PTS

Objective: To determine that the applicant—

1. Exhibits knowledge of the elements related to a maximum performance takeoff and climb.
2. Considers situations where this maneuver is recommended and factors related to takeoff and climb performance, including height/velocity information.
3. Maintains RPM within normal limits.
4. Utilizes proper control technique to initiate takeoff and forward climb airspeed attitude.
5. Utilizes the maximum available takeoff power.
6. After clearing all obstacles, transitions to normal climb attitude; airspeed, ±10 knots (for private) and ±5 knots (for commercial); and power setting.
7. Remains aware of the possibility of wind shear and/or wake turbulence.
8. Maintains proper ground track with crosswind correction, if necessary.

High Altitude (Running) Takeoff

Purpose

The purpose of practicing a running takeoff is to simulate a high-density altitude or high-gross-weight situation when a hover cannot be sustained.

Description

Clear the area around the helicopter to the right and left, in front and above. To simulate a high altitude condition, limit the amount of power you are able to use first by reducing the manifold pressure limit by 2". To make it even tougher, reduce each practice takeoff by 1" until you can no longer depart.

1. Start the takeoff by slowly raising the collective until the helicopter becomes light on its skids. While light on the skids, pause for a moment to neutralize all movements of the helicopter. Continue to slowly increase the collective until manifold pressure is 2" below noted hover power (for training). Apply forward cyclic to get the helicopter sliding forward on the surface. Maintain a straight ground track with lateral cyclic and heading with pedals.

2. As the aircraft gains effective translational lift (ETL), use slight back pressure on the cyclic to lift the helicopter off the ground. A small amount of lateral cyclic may be needed to correct for drift. When the helicopter lifts off the ground and the blades begin to cone, the RPM will increase, causing the governor to decrease the throttle and in turn, lower the power available. To counteract this, increase the collective to maintain the original power setting.

3. Continue to accelerate, remaining below 10 feet to stay in ground effect and within the height-velocity diagram until a minimum climb speed of at least 45 KIAS is reached.

4. At 50 feet of altitude, adjust manifold pressure to climb power (hover manifold pressure) and resume a normal climb at 60 KIAS.

Note: The student should never voluntarily place their aircraft in a situation that requires this maneuver.

Common Errors

- Too much forward cyclic.
- Failure to keep heading aligned with ground track.
- Exceeding manifold pressure limits.
- Failure to obtain ETL before departing the ground.
- Losing ETL once airborne.

Tips

Initially it will take a fair amount of cyclic to start the helicopter moving. Once it has begun, a reduction of forward cyclic may be necessary.

For practice, begin by setting your manifold limits to 2" below your maximum. As you gain proficiency, try subtracting an inch each time until the helicopter is no longer able to accelerate above ETL.

Be cautious of dynamic rollover, and always practice on smooth surfaces.

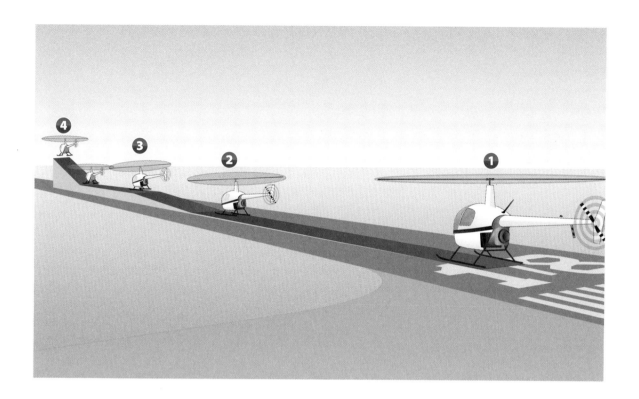

Private and Commercial PTS

Objective: To determine that the applicant—

1. Exhibits knowledge of the elements related to a rolling takeoff.
2. Considers situations where this maneuver is recommended and factors related to takeoff and climb performance, including height/velocity information.
3. Maintains RPM within normal limits.
4. Utilizes proper preparatory technique prior to initiating takeoff.
5. Initiates forward accelerating movement on the surface.
6. Transitions to a normal climb airspeed, ±10 knots (for private) or ±5 knots (for commercial), and power setting.
7. Remains aware of the possibility of wind shear and/or wake turbulence.
8. Maintains proper ground track with crosswind correction, if necessary.
9. Completes the prescribed checklist, if applicable.

High Altitude (Running) Landing

Purpose

The running landing maneuver is used to simulate an approach and landing when sufficient power for hovering is not available due to a high-density altitude, high gross weight, or partial engine malfunction (such as a failed magneto).

Description

On final approach, the helicopter should be headed into the wind at 60 KIAS and 300 feet AGL. When a shallow approach angle of 5 degrees is intercepted, begin the approach by lowering the collective to maintain the approach angle.

1 Begin a slow deceleration with aft cyclic, maintain the approach angle with the collective, and keep the aircraft in trim with the pedals. Crab the helicopter when above 50 feet AGL and use a slip below 50 feet AGL to align the aircraft with the ground track. It is important that the helicopter's skids are parallel with the ground track to avoid possible dynamic rollover.

2 Plan to smoothly land the helicopter at the point of intended touchdown while taking advantage of effective translational lift (ETL) by landing at or above ETL.

3 The helicopter may be in a slight nose-high position prior to ground contact. Level the helicopter by adding forward cyclic. Use collective inputs to ease the helicopter to the ground and to ensure a smooth landing.

4 After ground contact, maintain heading with the pedals and ground track with the cyclic. *Gently* lower the collective to slow the helicopter down. If the collective is lowered too rapidly, unanticipated yaw may occur, increasing the risk of dynamic rollover. Lowering the collective changes the amount of antitorque pedal needed, so a small amount of right pedal may be required to keep the skids parallel to the path of travel. In a Robinson R22, the helicopter may drift to the right due to translating tendency, and a small amount of lateral pressure to the left may be required for directional control. Do not apply any cyclic to help the helicopter slow down, but rather, use the friction from the skids to do so.

Common Errors

- Incorrect approach angle (too steep/shallow).
- Improper use of cyclic to control rate of closure.
- Failure to maintain directional control with the pedals.
- Loss of the additional lift with ETL.
- Landing the helicopter with a nose high/low attitude.
- Failure to maintain pedal control after touchdown.
- Failure to maintain ground track after touchdown.
- Drifting to the right after touchdown.

Tips

This maneuver is good practice for a limited-power situation and should not be rushed. Practice initially by limiting yourself on the amount of power (in a Robinson R22, keep it under 20") and then for each subsequent practice, take away 10% more to further limit yourself.

This maneuver should be done with precision. Pick an exact spot to make ground contact, but understand that you will roll/slide past it once on the ground.

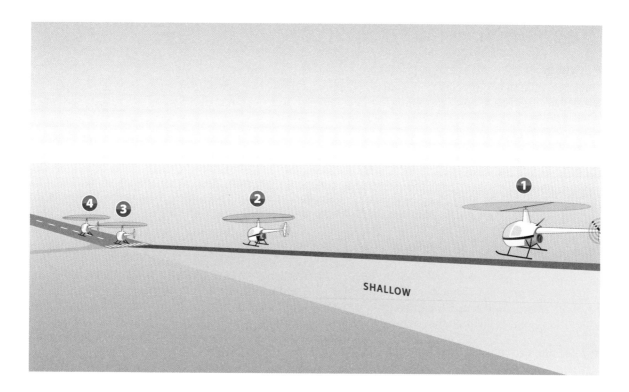

SHALLOW

Private and Commercial PTS

Objective: To determine that the applicant—

1. Exhibits knowledge of the elements related to shallow approach and running/roll-on landing, including the purpose of the maneuver; factors affecting performance data, including height/velocity information and the effect of landing surface texture.
2. Maintains RPM within normal limits.
3. Considers obstacles and other hazards.
4. Establishes and maintains the recommended approach angle and proper rate of closure.
5. Remains aware of the possibility of wind shear and/or wake turbulence.
6. Maintains proper ground track with crosswind correction, if necessary.
7. Maintains a speed that will take advantage of effective translational lift during surface contact, with landing gear parallel with the ground track.
8. Utilizes proper flight control technique after surface contact.
9. Completes the prescribed checklist, if applicable.

Steep Approach to a Hover

Purpose

The steep approach is used to transition from flight at altitude to a hover using a steeper-than-normal approach angle due to obstacles along the intended flight path. A steep approach is also used to avoid areas of turbulence around a pinnacle approach.

Description

1 On final approach, the helicopter should be headed into the wind, aligned with the point of intended touchdown, at 60 KIAS and 300 feet AGL. The collective controls the angle of approach, the cyclic controls the rate of closure and the path of flight, and the pedals control heading.

2 When passing the normal approach angle of 10 degrees, begin the approach by lowering the collective and applying aft cyclic to slow the helicopter. When the steep approach angle of 15 degrees is intercepted, continue lowering the collective so that the helicopter begins descending on the necessary approach angle. Coordinate right pedal for trim. Since this angle is steeper than a normal approach angle, the collective must be reduced more than for a normal approach. Reference the touchdown point on the windshield to determine changes in the approach angle.

3 Maintain a crab above 50 feet and a slip below 50 feet. Maintain the approach angle and rate of descent with the collective, the rate of closure with the cyclic, and trim with the pedals. Avoid high descent rates of more than 300 feet per minute at airspeeds below 30 KIAS because of the danger of settling with power.

4 Loss of ETL will occur higher above the ground during a steep approach, requiring an increase in collective to prevent settling. This action should be coordinated with left pedal for trim, and forward cyclic.

5 Terminate at a stabilized 3-foot hover by adding collective to arrest the rate of descent, left pedal for yaw control, and forward cyclic to level the helicopter. If you are unable to terminate to a 3-foot hover due to the increased power demands of arresting the descent, terminate the approach to a low hover height (between the ground and 1 foot) to avoid exceeding manifold pressure limits.

Common Errors

- Improper approach angle (collective).
- Improper rate of closure (cyclic).
- Improper pedal inputs with power changes.
- Failure to arrive at termination point at zero airspeed.
- Unable to determine location of loss of ETL.
- Rate of descent too high when below ETL.

Tips

Don't rush this maneuver, and don't fly the helicopter aggressively towards the ground. Plan on terminating to a hover at a specific point. If you are going to overshoot the spot, don't hesitate to perform a go-around. It's better to make a good decision early than to try to fix a bad approach during times of high power demands and when in close proximity to the ground.

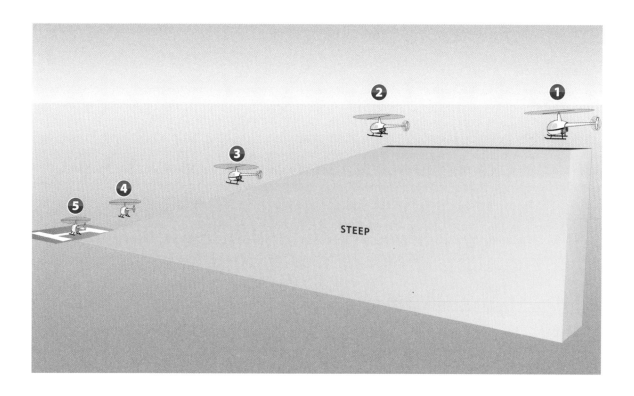

Private and Commercial PTS

Objective: To determine that the applicant—

1. Exhibits knowledge of the elements related to a steep approach.
2. Considers situations where this maneuver is recommended and factors related to a steep approach, including height/velocity information.
3. Considers the wind conditions, landing surface, and obstacles.
4. Selects a suitable termination point.
5. Establishes and maintains the recommended approach angle (15° maximum) and proper rate of closure.
6. Avoids situations that can result in settling-with-power.
7. Remains aware of the possibility of wind shear and/or wake turbulence.
8. Maintains proper ground track with crosswind correction, if necessary.
9. Arrives at the termination point, on the surface or at a stabilized hover, ±4 feet (for private) or ±2 feet (for commercial).

Steep Approach to the Surface

Purpose

The steep approach to the surface is used to accomplish an approach to the surface when loose snow or dusty surface conditions exist.

Description

This technique will provide the most favorable visibility conditions and reduce the possibility of debris ingestion by the engine, main rotor and/or tail rotor. Maintain the appropriate descent angle with the collective, heading with the pedals, and rate of closure with the cyclic.

 This approach is initiated in the same manner as the steep approach to a hover; however, instead of terminating at an altitude of 3 feet, the approach is continued until touchdown to the surface. Touchdown should occur smoothly, with the skids level, at zero ground speed.

Common Errors

- Improper approach angle (collective).
- Improper rate of closure (cyclic).
- Improper pedal inputs with power changes.
- Failure to arrive at termination point at zero airspeed.
- Rate of descent too high when at speeds below ETL.

Tips

It's better to make a good decision early than to try to fix a bad approach during times of high power demands and within close proximity to the ground.

This maneuver should be terminated at a specific point. If the helicopter is going to overshoot, don't hesitate to perform a go-around. Don't rush this maneuver, and don't fly the helicopter aggressively towards the ground.

Private and Commercial PTS

Objective: To determine that the applicant—

1. Exhibits knowledge of the elements related to a steep approach.
2. Considers situations where this maneuver is recommended and factors related to a steep approach, including height/velocity information.
3. Considers the wind conditions, landing surface, and obstacles.
4. Selects a suitable termination point.
5. Establishes and maintains the recommended approach angle (15° maximum) and proper rate of closure.
6. Avoids situations that can result in settling-with-power.
7. Remains aware of the possibility of wind shear and/or wake turbulence.
8. Maintains proper ground track with crosswind correction, if necessary.
9. Arrives at the termination point *on the surface*, ±4 feet (for private) or ±2 feet (for commercial).

Rapid Decelerations (Quick Stops)

Purpose

A rapid deceleration is used to simulate a condition in which a rapid decrease in forward airspeed is required, as in an aborted takeoff.

Description

Perform a normal takeoff into the wind. The quick stop should only be performed into the wind, as there is a high risk of settling with power in a downwind condition.

1 Once a minimum altitude of 40 feet is attained, apply additional forward cyclic to accelerate to 30–40 KIAS while maintaining altitude. Stabilize your helicopter at 40 feet and 40 KIAS.

2 Begin the quick stop by smoothly lowering the collective and simultaneously adding right pedal to maintain trim. Apply aft cyclic as needed to maintain entry altitude while rapidly decelerating the helicopter. Because the helicopter is operating on the back side of the power curve as airspeed is lost, it will begin to settle due to the increased power demand.

3 Once the helicopter starts to experience the loss of effective translational lift (ETL), allow it to settle towards the ground by adding forward cyclic to level flight attitude. Slowly increase the collective to control the angle and rate of descent. The angle of descent should be no greater than a steep approach.

4 With the loss of ETL, additional collective will be needed to maintain the rate of descent. Maintain heading with the pedals, and terminate at a stabilized 3-foot hover. Use caution to avoid terminating at a high hover or in an extreme tail-low attitude.

Common Errors

- Inability to maintain altitude during the initial flare.
- Improper pedal inputs that correspond to collective inputs.
- Improper collective and cyclic inputs.
- Failure to control rate of deceleration.
- Stopping forward motion in a tail-low attitude.
- Failure to maintain safe clearance over terrain.
- Excessive nose-high attitude.

Tips

This maneuver is helpful when learning about coordination. Be sure to lead rapid deceleration by lowering the collective. During the initial flare to slow the helicopter, the amount of decreased collective is directly proportional to the rate and amount of aft cyclic used. If the collective is lowered too aggressively, a large amount of aft cyclic will be needed to maintain the altitude.

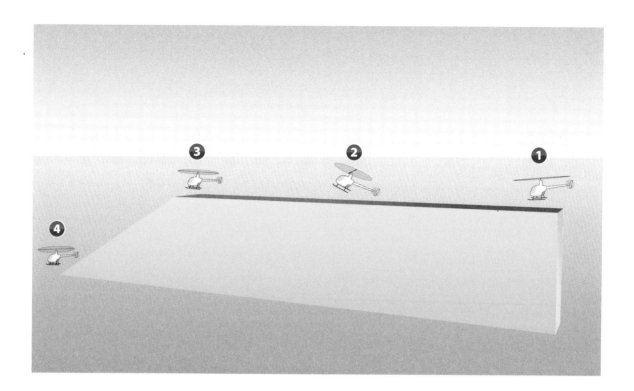

Private and Commercial PTS

Objective: To determine that the applicant—

1. Exhibits knowledge of the elements related to rapid deceleration.
2. Maintains RPM within normal limits.
3. Properly coordinates all controls throughout the execution of the maneuver.
4. Maintains an altitude that will permit safe clearance between the tail boom and the surface.
5. Decelerates and terminates in a stationary hover at the recommended hovering altitude.
6. Maintains heading throughout the maneuver, ±10° (for private) or ±5° (for commercial).

Chapter 5
Off-Airport Operations

Slope Operations

▨ Purpose

This maneuver is used to land on a sloping surface from a hover and to takeoff from a sloping surface to a hover.

▨ Description

Prior to conducting slope operations, you must be thoroughly familiar with dynamic rollover characteristics and mast bumping. Use a maximum slope angle of 5°. Always approach and depart the slope at a 45° angle to ensure tail rotor clearance from obstacles. Never turn your tail rotor into the slope. When entering and exiting the slope area, the pilot should visually check the area for the tail rotor, then announce, "tail clear."

Landing on a slope

1 Approach the slope at a 45-degree angle and once over the spot, perform a slow pedal turn to position the helicopter parallel with the slope at a stabilized 3-foot hover headed into the wind. When ready, slowly and slightly lower the collective to establish a slow rate of descent. Focus your eyes on a point at least 20 feet in front of the helicopter. Use your peripheral vision for control inputs; it is easy to have tunnel vision during periods of high stress.

2 When the upslope skid contacts the ground, stabilize all movement. Begin applying lateral cyclic gently in the direction of the slope (upslope) to hold the skid against the slope. Maintain heading with the pedals. Hold the one skid and hover momentarily while the helicopter is stabilized.

3 Lower collective slowly while simultaneously applying gentle lateral cyclic in the direction of the slope to hold the uphill skid in place. If at any time the cyclic hits the hard stop and no more cyclic travel is available before the downhill skid settles to the ground, abort the landing and pick a new slope. Slowly lower the collective all the way down to the hard stop.

4 Once the downhill skid settles to the ground and the collective is full down, slowly center the cyclic so the rotor disc is parallel with the slope. Be mindful of where the rotor disc is in relationship to the uphill slope. If passengers are to embark or disembark the helicopter, make sure they know the potential dangers of contacting the rotor disc.

Takeoff from a slope

The procedure for a slope takeoff is almost the exact reverse of that for a slope landing.

3 Apply lateral cyclic into the slope (upslope) and slowly begin to increase the collective. As the downslope skid becomes light, pause and neutralize any aircraft movement. Continue to slowly increase the collective while maintaining heading with the pedals. The uphill skid is now a pivot point, so be aware of potential dynamic rollover uphill.

2 When the downslope skid breaks ground and the aircraft begins to level, slowly begin to center the cyclic while simultaneously keeping the uphill skid held firmly on the ground. As a level attitude is reached, the cyclic should be approximately neutral and the helicopter will be in a light, one-skid hover.

1 Continue to increase the collective until the uphill skid breaks ground. Maintain position over the ground with the cyclic and heading with the pedals until a stabilized 3-foot hover is attained. Depart the slope area at a 45° angle and never turn your tail into the slope.

▨ Common Errors

- Rushing the maneuver.
- Improper selection of, approach to, or departure from the slope.
- Failure to consider wind effects.
- Turning tail towards the slope.
- Lowering downslope skid too fast.
- Allowing conditions that could lead to dynamic rollover.
- Improper heading control with pedals.

Tips

Relax, this maneuver is all about finesse. Rushing may result in overcontrolling the helicopter. A good exercise is to practice going from the full down position to a one-skid hover and then back to the full down position.

The uphill skid becomes a pivot point throughout this maneuver so be careful of the potential for dynamic rollover uphill. Use your peripheral vision for control inputs and avoid focusing on the ground directly in front of the helicopter. Keep your eyes focused at least 20 feet out in front.

This maneuver uses large power changes and it's easy to become too focused on the rolling moment of the helicopter, and therefore forget to correct any heading changes with the pedals.

Private and Commercial PTS

Objective: To determine that the applicant—

1. Exhibits knowledge of the elements related to slope operations.
2. Selects a suitable slope, approach, and direction considering wind effect, obstacles, dynamic rollover avoidance, and discharging passengers.
3. Properly moves toward the slope.
4. Maintains RPM within normal limits.
5. Makes a smooth positive descent to touch the upslope skid on the sloping surface.
6. Maintains positive control while lowering the downslope skid or landing gear to touchdown.
7. Recognizes if slope is too steep and abandons the operation prior to reaching cyclic control stops.
8. Makes a smooth transition from the slope to a stabilized hover parallel to the slope.
9. Properly moves away from the slope.
10. Maintains the specified heading throughout the operation, ±10° (for private) or ±5° (for commercial).

High/Low Reconnaissance

Purpose

The reconnaissance maneuver is used to determine the suitability and conditions for landing at an unfamiliar location.

Description

Wind plays a major role in determining the direction from which to make the approach. To help you discover where the wind is coming from, hold a constant bank angle during your first turn and correspond your ground track to what a "normal" circular pattern would be. The difference between them will show you where the wind is coming from.

1 Start the high reconnaissance maneuver at approximately 500 feet AGL above the point of intended landing. Roll into the turn by adding lateral cyclic. Make the turn on the pilot's side to help with visibility. Maintain a constant distance from the point of intended landing. During the high orbit determine the direction and velocity of the wind by recognizing when the turn is made steeper and shallower; the steepest turn will be made when turning while on downwind. Keep the airspeed above 60 KIAS during the high reconnaissance.

While on the high reconnaissance, visualize your intended path of ingress (final approach) and egress (departure path). Also look for obstacles, possible turbulence causes (high buildings or tall trees), forced landing areas, and power lines or any other wires.

2 To enter the low reconnaissance maneuver from high reconnaissance, descend to 300 feet AGL above the point of intended landing, maintaining an airspeed above 45 KIAS. Continue circling the point of intended landing to confirm what you learned during the high reconnaissance, keeping the landing zone in view at all times.

Take a closer look at the landing zone itself. Determine the type of surface, whether or not a slope is involved, and if the zone contains any other obstacles that would prevent you from landing safely. Check for loose debris, dust, snow, wood or dirt, and anything that could cause a loss of visibility or damage to the helicopter. Do not allow the helicopter to lose altitude or to sustain an excessive loss of airspeed while performing this maneuver.

Common Errors

- Failure to perform proper reconnaissance.
- Misjudgment of the wind.
- Misjudgment of the mechanical turbulence in and around the landing zone.
- Turning the wrong direction to view the site.
- Failure to control the airspeed during the reconnaissance.
- Failure to hold altitude during the reconnaissance.

Tips

This is an advanced maneuver that should only be practiced with a certified flight instructor on board. It is your responsibility as pilot-in-command to ensure the safe operation of the helicopter, so do not allow yourself to be rushed. Take as much time as necessary to complete a safe and thorough reconnaissance. If you are still unsure as to the suitability of the landing zone after the low reconnaissance, try a low approach to help make a final decision. Select an approach and departure into the wind and fly a normal approach down to 100 feet AGL. Maintain altitude and airspeed and use this last opportunity to secure a safe landing.

Private and Commercial PTS

This maneuver is part of any off-airport landing and is closely related to pinnacle and confined area operational procedures. The PTS contain no specific standards regarding reconnaissance; however, use the guidance of your certified flight instructor for standards.

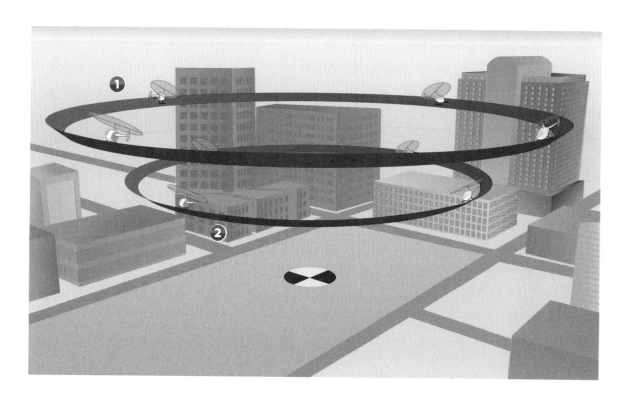

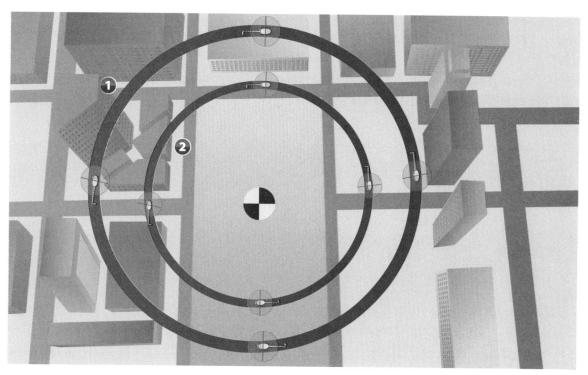

Confined Area Operations

Purpose

The confined area maneuver is used to land or takeoff from an area where the helicopter operation is limited by some type of obstruction.

Description

1 The confined area approach begins with a high reconnaissance to determine the suitability of an area for landing. It is normally conducted at an altitude of 500 feet AGL and 60 KIAS airspeed. Plan the approach with the following considerations: wind direction and speed; the most suitable flight paths into and out of the area with particular consideration given to forced landing areas; the size of barriers; and intended point of touchdown.

2 Perform high and low reconnaissance maneuvers in order to determine the suitability of the landing zone.

3 Once you feel the area is safe for landing, extend the downwind leg in preparation for the final approach. Be sure to keep the landing zone in sight at all times. Plan the approach to be as close to normal as possible. However, the approach angle should be steep enough to permit clearance from any obstacles. Typically, the approach angle should not be greater than a steep approach.

4 To determine the landing zone by using the "two-thirds, one-third" rule, use $\frac{2}{3}$ of the available area and leave $\frac{1}{3}$ of the area for overshooting your approach points. The decision to make the landing or go-around must be made before losing ETL. Terminate the approach to a hover unless surface conditions require termination on the surface. At all times during the approach, be on the lookout for wires and other hard-to-see obstacles.

5 Perform a ground reconnaissance before takeoff to determine the point from which to initiate the takeoff. Observe wind conditions and decide the best way to get from the landing point to the proposed takeoff path. This reconnaissance can be made from the cockpit or by conducting a walk around the area after the helicopter is shut down. Prior to takeoff, perform a power check and complete the before-takeoff checklist, then clear aircraft right, left, front and overhead. Perform a maximum performance takeoff to clear barriers. After clearing obstacles, reduce power to a normal climb airspeed and rate of climb.

Common Errors

- Failure to conduct a complete high/low reconnaissance.
- Failure to track selected approach path or fly an acceptable approach angle and rate of closure.
- Inadequate planning to ensure obstacle clearance during the approach or departure.
- Failure to consider emergency forced landing areas.
- Failure to select a definite termination point during the low reconnaissance.
- Failure to consider the effect of wind direction, wind speed, turbulence, or loss of ETL during the approach.
- Improper takeoff and climb technique for existing conditions
- Fixation on instruments instead of on your surroundings.

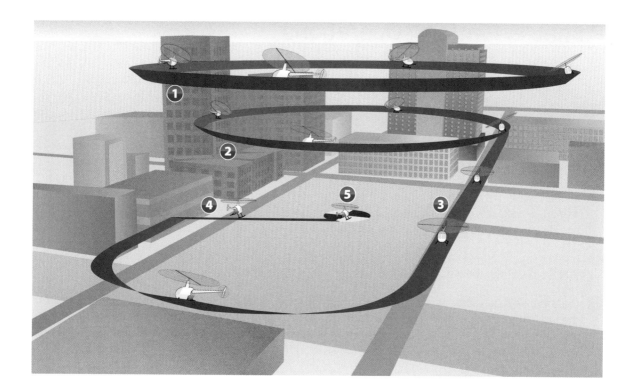

Tips

This is an advanced maneuver that should be practiced only with a certified flight instructor on board. If you are still unsure of the landing zone, try a low approach with a departure into the wind and fly a normal approach down to 100 feet AGL. Maintain altitude and airspeed, and this last reconnaissance will allow you to further determine the suitability of the landing zone. Below 100 feet AGL, use the shallowest possible approach given your local conditions with regard to obstacles and wind.

Private and Commercial PTS:

Objective: To determine that the applicant—

1. Exhibits knowledge of the elements related to confined area operations.
2. Accomplishes a proper high and low reconnaissance.
3. Selects a suitable approach path, termination point, and departure path.
4. Tracks the selected approach path at an acceptable approach angle and rate of closure to the termination point.
5. Maintains RPM within normal limits.
6. Avoids situations that can result in settling-with-power.
7. Terminates at a hover or on the surface, as conditions allow.
8. Accomplishes a proper ground reconnaissance.
9. Selects a suitable takeoff point and considers factors affecting takeoff and climb performance under various conditions.

Pinnacle/Platform Operations

Purpose

Pinnacle or platform operations are used to land and takeoff from an area where the terrain drops away steeply on one or more sides.

Description

1 Pinnacle landing begins with a high reconnaissance to collect as much information as possible about the conditions and terrain. This includes wind direction and velocity, obstructions that could cause turbulence, obstacles that affect the approach path and landing, forced landing areas, terrain, and any other factors that influence the approach and landing. The high reconnaissance should be conducted from 500 feet AGL at a safe airspeed.

2 Use the low reconnaissance to confirm everything seen on the high reconnaissance and also to double-check the wind and turbulence conditions at the landing site.

3 Once you've determined that the area is safe for landing, extend the downwind leg in preparation for the final approach. Be sure to keep the landing spot in sight at all times. The approach angle should be a normal-to-steep approach, dictated by the velocity of the wind. The greater the wind, the steeper the approach angle; in the case of a no-wind situation, a normal approach angle can be used.

4 Throughout the approach, evaluate the landing area for suitability. If leeward downdrafts are encountered, you may have to make an immediate go-around to avoid being forced into the rising terrain.

5 Before takeoff, conduct a ground reconnaissance to evaluate the area. This includes checking the wind direction and velocity, the terrain, and the best route of flight during the takeoff and departure. Conduct a normal takeoff from hover unless obstacles exist. In that case, make a maximum performance takeoff from the surface to clear the obstacles. During the departure, give priority to gaining airspeed rather than altitude in order to facilitate an autorotation, should it become necessary.

Common Errors

- Failure to conduct a high/low reconnaissance.
- Failure to fly the selected approach path, angle, or rate of closure.
- Inadequate planning to ensure obstacle clearance during approach or departure.
- Failure to consider emergency landing locations.
- Failure to select a termination point during the high reconnaissance.
- Failure to change the termination point if necessary.
- Failure to consider the effect of wind direction, wind speed, turbulence or loss of ETL during approach.
- Improper takeoff and climb technique for existing conditions.

Tips

This maneuver is an advanced maneuver that should be practiced only with a certified flight instructor on board. If you are still unsure as to the suitability of the landing zone following the low reconnaissance, try a low approach to help make a final decision. Select an approach and departure into the wind and fly a normal approach down to 100 feet AGL. Maintain altitude and airspeed and use this last opportunity to secure a safe landing. Use the shallowest approach possible given your local wind conditions.

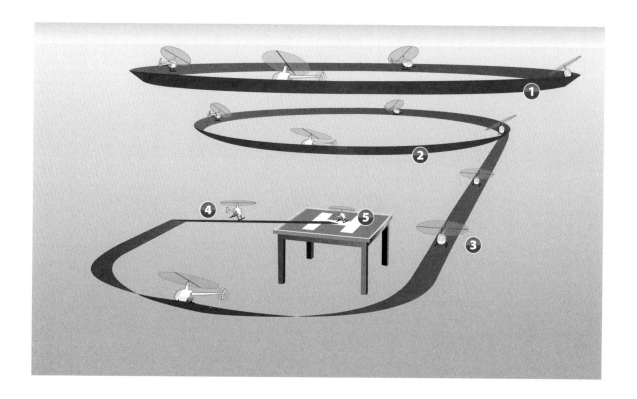

Private and Commercial PTS

Objective: To determine that the applicant—

1. Exhibits knowledge of the elements related to pinnacle/platform operations.
2. Accomplishes a proper high and low reconnaissance.
3. Selects a suitable approach path, termination point, and departure path.
4. Tracks the selected approach path at an acceptable approach angle and rate of closure to the termination point.
5. Maintains RPM within normal limits.
6. Terminates at a hover or on the surface, as conditions allow.
7. Accomplishes a proper ground reconnaissance.
8. Selects a suitable takeoff point and considers factors affecting takeoff and climb performance under various conditions.

Chapter 6
Emergency Operations

Straight-In Autorotation with Power Recovery

Purpose

The straight-in autorotation is used to simulate safely landing the helicopter with a complete power loss.

Description

⚠ **CAUTION:** Never practice autorotations without a certified flight instructor on board the aircraft!

Because the angle of approach will increase in high-wind situations, the entry point may need to be varied to "hit" the spot. (Robinson R22 tip: Try using the reference point of halfway between the trim strings and the top of the instrument console.)

❶ The entry

From level flight of 70 KIAS, at or above 500 feet AGL, and heading into the wind, smoothly lower the collective full down, then reduce the throttle to idle. Coordinate the collective movement with the right pedal for trim and aft cyclic to establish and maintain a 65 KIAS attitude. The RPM needles will split, establishing an autorotative descent. Cross-check the helicopter's attitude, trim, rotor RPM and airspeed. A slight increase in collective will be necessary to maintain rotor RPM in the green if high gross weight condition exists. The throttle should be retarded to maintain the engine RPM at or below 80% at all times, but expect the engine RPM to increase if the collective is raised. Keep the engine RPM at idle by holding the throttle in the idle position.

❷ The glide

After establishing the descent, the airspeed should be 65 KIAS and this attitude should be maintained throughout the glide. During straight-in autorotative glides, aft cyclic movements will cause an increase in rotor RPM which can be counteracted by a small increase in collective. If the collective is increased to control the rotor RPM, retard the throttle slightly to prevent the correlator from joining the needles. Avoid a large collective increase, which will result in a rapid decay of rotor RPM and lead to "chasing the RPM." Maintain rotor RPM in the green and keep the aircraft in trim during the glide. Below 100 feet AGL, maintain aircraft alignment with a slip. Use the cyclic to hold a constant 65 KIAS attitude. Avoid looking straight down in front of the aircraft. Continually cross-check attitude, trim, rotor RPM, and airspeed.

❸ The flare

At approximately 40 feet AGL, begin the flare with aft cyclic to reduce forward airspeed and to decrease the rate of descent. The amount of flare will depend on wind conditions and gross weight and should gradually be increased so that ground speed and rate of descent are significantly decreased. Too much flare will cause the helicopter to balloon up, resulting in a high vertical descent as airspeed is lost. Prior to the bottom of the flair, increase the throttle to normal operating speeds (Robinson R22 pilots: Increase the throttle above 80% and allow the governor to manage the throttle up to 104%. Do this once the flare has been established to help ensure the engine and rotor RPM needles meet up at 104%.)

❹ The power recovery

At a skid height of approximately 8 to 10 feet, begin to level the helicopter with forward cyclic. Extreme caution should be used to avoid an excessive nose-high/tail-low attitude below 10 feet. Just prior to achieving a level attitude and with the nose still slightly up, increase the collective while maintaining heading with the left pedal. Verify the RPM is at normal operating speeds. Do not allow the helicopter to descend below 3 feet during the power recovery.

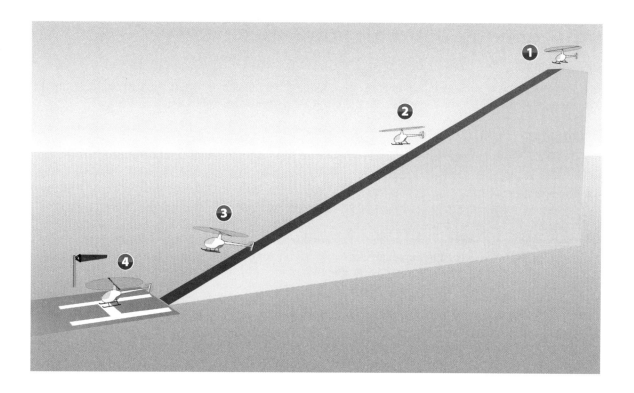

Common Errors

- Improper engine and rotor RPM control.
- Uncoordinated flight controls.
- Improper attitude and airspeed during descent.
- Improper judgment and technique during termination.
- Failure to maintain correct heading with pedals.
- Diving towards the ground.
- Chasing RPM and airspeed.
- Fixation on one part of the scan.
- Ground track not followed.

Tips

It is extremely important to enter the maneuver with proper level attitude, as this will provide a better chance of success for the remainder of the maneuver. When entering the autorotation, look outside at the horizon during the entry. When lowering the collective, a small amount of aft cyclic will be needed to maintain the attitude. Don't forget to add left pedal at the end of the autorotation when you are increasing the collective.

Private and Commercial PTS

Objective: To determine that the applicant—

1. Exhibits knowledge of the elements related to a straight-in autorotation terminating with a power recovery to a hover.
2. Selects a suitable touchdown area.
3. Initiates the maneuver at the proper point.
4. Establishes proper aircraft trim and autorotation airspeed, ±5 knots.
5. Maintains rotor RPM within normal limits.
6. Compensates for wind speed and direction as necessary to avoid undershooting or overshooting the selected landing area.
7. Utilizes proper deceleration and collective pitch application to a hover.
8. Comes to a hover within 200 feet (for private) or 100 feet (for commercial) of a designated point.

180° Autorotation with Power Recovery

Purpose

The purpose of this maneuver is to simulate safely landing the helicopter by turning 180 degrees with a complete power loss. This will allow for a turn into the wind from a downwind situation.

Description

⚠ **CAUTION:** Never practice autorotations without a certified flight instructor on board the aircraft!

1 The entry

Establish the aircraft on downwind at 70 KIAS and 700 feet AGL. When abeam the intended touchdown point, enter the autorotation by smoothly but firmly lowering the collective full down and then reducing the throttle by rolling it off. The needles will split, establishing an autorotation. When lowering the collective, simultaneously apply right pedal for trim and aft cyclic to establish a 65 KIAS attitude. Cross-check the helicopter's attitude, trim, rotor RPM, and airspeed.

2 The glide

After establishing the glide to the proper attitude (65 KIAS attitude), begin a 180-degree turn by adding lateral cyclic in the direction of the turn. The proper angle of bank will be determined by wind velocity, but use caution to avoid an excessively steep turn. The steeper the turn, the more the RPM will increase due to Coriolis effect in the main rotor blades. Throughout the turn, it is important to maintain the proper attitude and airspeed with the cyclic and to keep the aircraft in trim. Changes in the aircraft's attitude and the angle of bank will cause corresponding change in rotor RPM. Adjust the collective as necessary in the turn to maintain rotor RPM in the green. Raise the collective to lower RPM, and lower the collective to raise RPM. Continually cross-check the rotor RPM when maneuvering in autorotative turns as the low inertia rotor system can allow rapid increases in rotor RPM. The turn should be completed and the helicopter aligned with the intended touchdown area prior to passing through 100 feet AGL. If the collective has been increased to load the rotor during the turn, it must to be lowered on roll out to prevent decay in RPM.

3 The flare

At approximately 40 feet AGL, begin the flare with the cyclic to reduce forward airspeed and to decrease the rate of descent. The amount of flare will depend on wind conditions and gross weight and should gradually be increased so that ground speed and rate of descent are significantly decreased. Too much flare will cause the helicopter to balloon up, resulting in a high vertical descent as airspeed is lost. Prior to the bottom of the flare, increase the throttle to normal operating speeds (Robinson R22 pilots: Increase the throttle above 80% and allow the governor to manage the throttle up to 104%. Do this once the flare has been established to help ensure the engine and rotor RPM needles meet up at 104%.)

4 The power recovery

At a skid height of approximately 8 to 10 feet, begin to level the helicopter with forward cyclic. Extreme caution should be used to avoid an excessive nose-high/tail-low attitude below 10 feet. Just prior to achieving a level attitude and with the nose still slightly up, increase the collective maintaining heading with left pedal. Verify the RPM is at normal operating speeds. Do not allow the helicopter to descend below 3 feet during the power recovery.

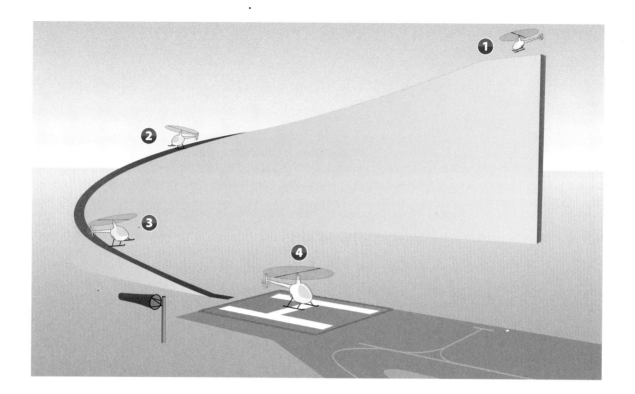

Common Errors

- Excessive RPM build during the turn.
- Allowing the nose to drop during the turn.
- Allowing the nose to climb during the turn.
- Improper engine and rotor RPM control (chasing airspeed and/or RPM).
- Uncoordinated flight controls (out of trim).
- Improper judgment and technique during termination.
- Failure to maintain correct heading with pedals during the turn and recovery.

Tips

Entering the maneuver with proper level attitude is extremely important and will provide a better chance of success for the remainder of the maneuver. When entering the autorotation, look outside at the horizon during the entry. When lowering the collective, a small amount of aft cyclic will be needed to maintain the attitude. Don't forget to add left pedal at the end of the autorotation when you are increasing the collective.

Private and Commercial PTS

Objective: To determine that the applicant—

1. Exhibits knowledge of the elements related to a 180° autorotation terminating with a power recovery to a hover.
2. Selects a suitable touchdown area.
3. Initiates the maneuver at the proper point.
4. Establishes proper aircraft trim and autorotation airspeed, ±5 knots.
5. Maintains rotor RPM within normal limits.
6. Compensates for wind speed and direction as necessary to avoid undershooting or overshooting the selected landing area.
7. Utilizes proper deceleration and collective pitch application to a hover.
8. Comes to a hover within 200 feet (for private) or 100 feet (for commercial) of a designated point.

Power Failure at a Hover (Hovering Autorotation)

Purpose

The power failure at a hover maneuver is used to simulate landing the helicopter from a hover with a complete power failure.

Description

Practice rolling the throttle off when on the surface using a countdown of "3, 2, 1, roll." The throttle should be rolled off in about one second; be cautious of "snapping" the throttle off quickly. Try saying out loud: "3, 2, 1, one-one thousand." This auditory practice will help to slow the maneuver down both for the instructor and the student.

---

1 Begin from a stabilized 3-foot hover at flight idle, governor off, over level terrain, and headed into the wind. If necessary, reposition your left hand so the throttle can easily be rolled off into the override position. Firmly roll the throttle into the spring-loaded override while simultaneously adding right pedal to maintain heading. The loss of tail rotor thrust will cause a left drift when the throttle is rolled off. Compensate for this drift with right lateral cyclic. Use caution not to raise or lower the collective when rolling off the throttle. Be aware that as the helicopter loses RPM the low RPM warning system will be on (light and horn).

---

2 When the aircraft has settled to approximately 1 foot, fully increase the collective to cushion the landing while continuing to hold the throttle firmly in the spring-loaded override position. As the skids touchdown, apply slight forward cyclic. Once firmly on the ground, lower the collective full down.

⚠️ **CAUTION:** Avoid any sideward or rearward movement on touchdown to prevent the possibility of a rollover.

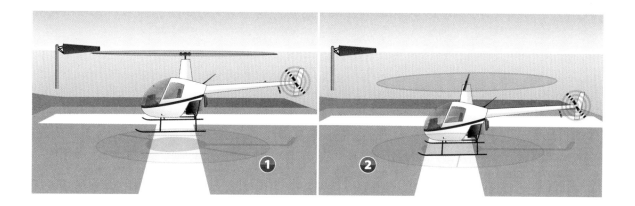

Common Errors

- Failure to maintain heading.
- Failure to compensate for drift prior to touchdown.
- Improper application of collective pitch.
- Failure to touchdown in a level attitude.
- Too much corrective right lateral cyclic.

Tips

When first learning this maneuver, it may be helpful to keep 3 to 5 KIAS of forward speed. This focuses attention on keeping the helicopter straight down the taxiway and should eliminate most if not all sideward or rearward movement. Also try starting at a hover height of 6 inches and work your way up to your maximum of 3 feet.

Private and Commercial PTS

Objective: To determine that the applicant—

1. Exhibits knowledge of the elements related to power failure at a hover.
2. Determines that the terrain below the aircraft is suitable for a safe touchdown.
3. Performs autorotation from a stationary or forward hover into the wind at recommended altitude, and RPM, while maintaining established heading, ±10° (for private) or ±5° (for commercial).
4. Touches down with minimum sideward movement, and no rearward movement.
5. Exhibits orientation, division of attention, and proper planning.

Power Failure at Altitude (Forced Landings)

Purpose

This maneuver is used to simulate an emergency situation and develop the student's reaction time, planning, and judgment in case of a power failure at altitude.

Description

1 During cruise flight with the student at the controls, the instructor will initiate the forced landing by announcing "engine failure" and rolling the throttle down slightly to simulate aircraft yaw. The instructor should *never* "chop" the throttle.

2 The student will immediately lower the collective full down and coordinate the right pedal for trim and aft cyclic to maintain attitude. This should be accomplished quickly enough to prevent the rotor RPM from decaying below 90%. As the rotor RPM builds back into the green, increase the collective as necessary to maintain rotor RPM in the green (hold the throttle against the detent position). Once established in an autorotative descent, select an intended landing area.

3 Maneuver the helicopter as necessary to align the aircraft with the intended landing area, generally headed into the wind. If necessary, use changes of the collective and cyclic to maintain the rotor RPM in green arc while maneuvering. Adjust the airspeed to 65 KIAS.

4 Prior to passing through 100 feet, align the aircraft with the touchdown area, at 65 KIAS, with rotor RPM in the green range and the aircraft in trim. Execute a termination with power recovery as with a straight-in autorotation, or an immediate power recovery, as directed by the instructor.

⚠️ **CAUTION:** Instructors should never "chop" or rapidly roll the throttle all the way down.

Common Errors

- Failure to recognize the emergency.
- Failure to maintain proper rotor RPM.
- Poor selection of landing sites or fixation on one site.
- Improper attitude during auto entry and descent.
- Incorrect use of flight controls during power recovery.

Tips

Instructors should pull full carb heat before this maneuver because the collective should be lowered well below 18" manifold pressure. This is a good teaching point for instructors to ensure the student is always thinking of where to land in the event of an engine failure. Sometimes the best spot is not the one directly in front of you.

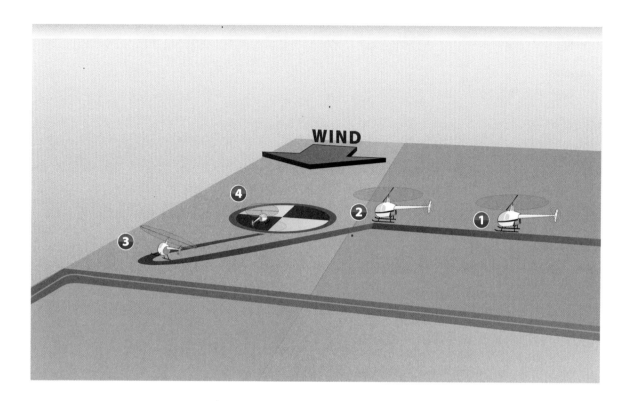

Private and Commercial PTS

Objective: To determine that the applicant—

1. Exhibits knowledge of the elements related to power failure at altitude.
2. Establishes an autorotation and selects a suitable landing area.
3. Establishes proper aircraft trim and autorotation airspeed, ±5 knots.
4. Maintains rotor RPM within normal limits.
5. Compensates for wind speed and direction as necessary to avoid undershooting or overshooting the selected landing area.
6. Terminates approach with a power recovery at a safe altitude when directed by the examiner.

Low Rotor RPM Recognition and Recovery

Purpose

To recognize and recover from low rotor RPM.

Description

This maneuver should only be practiced with an instructor on board the helicopter. The instructor will turn the governor off and slowly decrease the throttle to 95% RPM. The low RPM condition will be recognized by:

1. A noticeable decrease in engine noise.

2. Aircraft vibration and cyclic stick shake.

3. The low rotor RPM warning horn and light will engage (R22 pilots: this will occur at approximately 97% RPM).

4. The instructor should demonstrate the further increase in vibration and decrease in engine noise by decreasing the RPM to 90% RPM. This is to show that the helicopter is able to continue to fly even at low RPM settings. However, great care should be exercised when operating at low RPM settings.

1 Upon recognizing the low RPM condition, simultaneously add throttle and lower the collective to regain operating RPM. A gentle aft cyclic movement will help the recovery, but the primary recovery controls are the collective and throttle. Avoid any forward cyclic input, which will inhibit RPM recovery.

2 Once RPM is regained, slowly raise the collective to reduce the sink rate while closely monitoring the RPM.

3 Once the sink rate has been eliminated, raise the collective and climb back to previous altitude to fully recover from the low RPM situation.

⚠ **CAUTION:** Never practice low RPM recovery without a certified flight instructor on board.

Common Errors

- Failure to recognize conditions that are conducive to development of low rotor RPM.
- Failure to detect the development of low rotor RPM and to initiate prompt corrective action.
- Improper use of controls (by increasing collective to stop descent).
- Over-speeding engine and rotor RPM by adding too much throttle.

Tips

On the ground, practice the throttle control a few times with the governor off to familiarize yourself with throttle travel. Then, in the air with your instructor, practice slowly rolling the throttle down to 95% and back up to normal speed (R22 pilots—104%).

You can also hear the decrease/increase of the RPM and pay attention to the yaw movement of the nose.

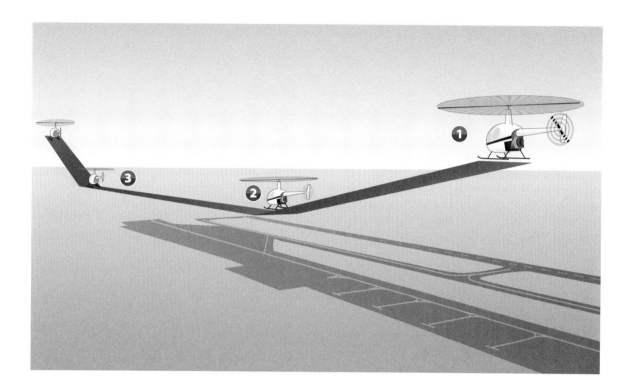

Private and Commercial PTS

Objective: To determine that the applicant—

1. Exhibits knowledge of the elements related to low rotor RPM recovery, including the combination of conditions that are likely to lead to this situation.

2. Detects the development of low rotor RPM and initiates prompt corrective action.

3. Utilizes the appropriate recovery procedure.

Settling-With-Power

Purpose

This maneuver demonstrates the dangerous results of operating at low airspeeds, moderate to high power settings, and high rates of descent.

Description

Settling-with-power is most dangerous when it happens at relatively low altitudes. The maneuvers that most commonly can result in settling occur during a steep approach with a tail wind, or an out-of-ground-effect (OGE) hover without precise altitude control.

This maneuver should be demonstrated at an altitude that will allow recovery to be completed *no less than 1,000 feet AGL*. Settling-with-power is a condition in which the helicopter descends vertically at a high rate of speed even though power is being used. This condition is also described as vortex ring state.

Three (3) conditions MUST exist to create this dangerous situation:

1. Airspeed must be less than effective translational lift.
2. You must be using 20–100% of engine available power.
3. Near vertical descent of at least 300 feet per minute.

---

1 From a stabilized OGE hover, begin to lower the collective to establish a sink rate of at least 300 feet per minute or more. The aircraft will begin to vibrate. This is the beginning of settling with power. Application of additional up collective will increase the vibration and sink rate. Once the condition is well developed, a rate-of-sink in excess of *2,000 feet per minute* can result.

---

2 A recovery should be initiated at the first sign of a rapid increase in the rate of descent on the vertical speed indicator (VSI) or a sensation of falling. To recover, simultaneously apply forward cyclic to increase airspeed while lowering the collective (if altitude permits). Two indications that you are out of vortex ring state are that the trim strings will straighten up with the flow of air over the fuselage and the airspeed indicator will rapidly increase from near zero to your indicated airspeed. At this point the helicopter is out of settling with power but may still be in a descent.

---

3 If the collective was lowered to establish a sink rate, the collective should be raised to a normal climb power setting to help arrest the rate of descent. The raising of the collective and increase in airspeed up to the V_Y will help facilitate the recovery. The recovery is complete when the aircraft accelerates to the normal climbing airspeed and a normal climb is established on the VSI.

⚠ **CAUTION:** Never practice recovery from settling-with-power without a certified flight instructor on board the helicopter.

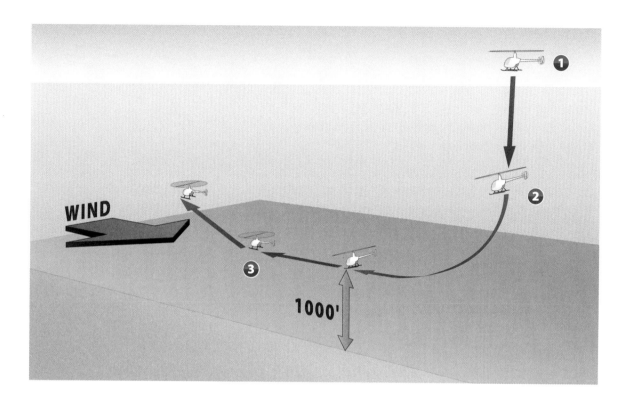

Common Errors

- Failure to recognize conditions that are conducive to development of settling-with-power.
- Failure to detect first indications of settling-with-power.
- Adding too much forward cyclic.
- Flying out of trim after the helicopter has recovered.

Tips

Altitude is key for this practice maneuver. The more altitude you have, the safer you are. If you are in a strong headwind situation, rearward flight in relation to the ground may be necessary to lose ETL.

Private and Commercial PTS

Objective: To determine that the applicant—

1. Exhibits knowledge of the elements related to settling-with-power.
2. Selects an altitude that will allow recovery to be completed no less than 1,000 feet AGL or, if applicable, the manufacturer's recommended altitude, whichever is higher.
3. Promptly recognizes and recovers at the onset of settling-with-power.
4. Utilizes the appropriate recovery procedure.

Tail Rotor Failure

Purpose

To become familiar with the recognition of the following types of tail rotor failures and the techniques used to perform a proper landing for each:

1. Tail rotor failure during hover.
2. Tail rotor failure during forward flight.
   A. Complete loss of tail rotor function and component parts (catastrophic failure).
   B. Loss of antitorque pedal function (neutral pedal).
   C. Loss of antitorque pedal function (stuck left pedal).
   D. Loss of antitorque pedal function (stuck right pedal).

Description

Each manufacturer has recommended recovery techniques for each scenario. Be sure to familiarize yourself with the emergency procedures located in the POH. Usually when there is a loss of tail rotor failure, the helicopter should be placed in autorotation. However, in the case of a stuck pedal there are some techniques to help in safely landing the helicopter. These examples assume a counterclockwise rotation of the main rotor.

Never practice tail rotor failures without a thorough preflight briefing and a certifiied flight instructor on board the helicopter.

During Hover

1 Failure is usually indicated by a right yaw that cannot be stopped by applying left pedal. Immediately close throttle and perform a hovering power-off landing autorotation. Keep the helicopter level with the cyclic and increase the collective just before touchdown to cushion landing.

Failure During Flight

2 Complete loss of tail rotor function and component parts is the most serious form of tail rotor failure. It is usually indicated by a right yaw and extremely nose-low attitude because of the change of CG. Immediately close the throttle and perform an autorotation. If there are no suitable places to land, you may achieve forward flight with lower power settings and by using the vertical fin to help with directional control.

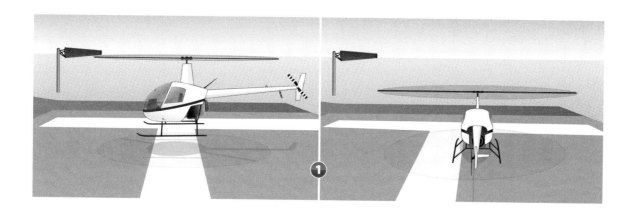

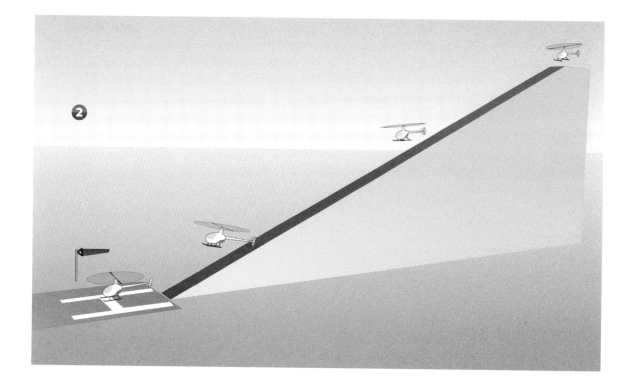

Loss of Function (Stuck Pedals Left, Right, or Neutral)

This malfunction can occur if the pedal controls between the tail rotor gearbox and the pedals jam or break. The tail rotor blades will be operating normally in whichever position they're stuck in and the pitch cannot be changed. Each scenario assumes that you have determined that the pedals will not move and you still have engine power.

There are three scenarios in which a pedal could be stuck: Stuck neutral, stuck left and stuck right.

3 **Stuck neutral**—When flying at normal speeds the pedals are usually in a neutral position. When the helicopter is slowed to speeds less than ETL, the requirement for left pedal becomes greater. A shallow-approach running landing at speeds greater than ETL is required to safely land the helicopter. As the helicopter slows, a reduction in collective/throttle is required to maintain heading. Do not apply any aft cyclic to help the helicopter slow down, but rather use the friction of the skids to slow the helicopter.

4 **Stuck left**—Under high power settings more left pedal is required. This is true when slowing the helicopter down below ETL. As the helicopter slows, raise the collective and try to hover the helicopter. If the helicopter continues to rotate to the left, slowly lower the collective and try to place the helicopter on the ground as level as possible. With the helicopter slowly rotating on the ground, gradual lowering of the collective may not slow the rotation, but friction between the skids and the surface will. Continue to lower the collective until it is in the full down position and then reduce the throttle. Make every effort to level the helicopter with the cyclic.

5 **Stuck right**—Because of the increased demands for the left pedal as the helicopter drops below ETL, perform a power-on running landing with airspeed above ETL. Once over the touchdown zone if the helicopter is still in a nose right yaw, slowly roll throttle down to line up the nose of the helicopter with the runway. Once aligned, slowly lower the collective to allow the helicopter to touch the ground with forward speed. Then slowly lower the collective to increase the friction between the surface and the skid shoes. Allow the friction to slow the helicopter while maintaining directional control with the throttle.

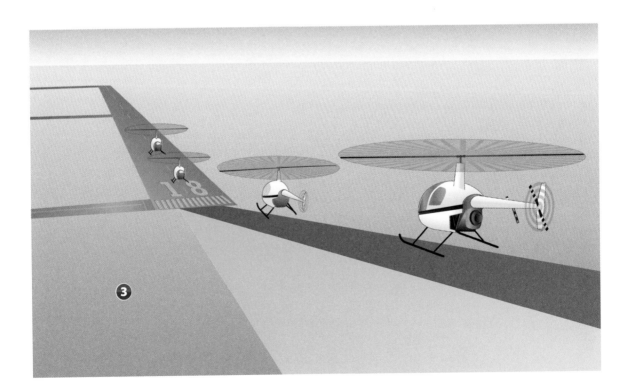

Common Errors

- Poor selection of safe landing site.
- Improper throttle or collective control to counter condition.
- Inability to control aircraft heading.
- Failing to level the helicopter with the cyclic.
- Failure to land evenly on all skid shoes simultaneously.

Tips

Have your instructor simulate stuck pedals and try different approach speeds and angles to see what works best in your helicopter. Remember that each helicopter is different and may respond differently. The amount of stuck pedal will also dictate how much corrective control inputs are needed.

Using crosswind approaches will help in a stuck-right or a stuck-left pedal scenario. A left quartering crosswind can be helpful in a stuck-right pedal scenario, as it will increase the effectiveness of the vertical stabilizer and help align the nose of the helicopter with the runway/taxiway. Likewise, a right quartering crosswind will aid in a stuck-left pedal scenario.

For counterclockwise rotating American helicopters, extending the index finger on the hand controlling the throttle will aid in recognizing the direction of yaw. Increasing throttle will point your finger to the right, resulting in a right yaw. Decreasing throttle will point your finger to the left, resulting in a left yaw.

Private PTS

Objective: To determine that the applicant—

1. Exhibits knowledge of the elements related to antitorque system failure by describing:
   a) The aerodynamic indications of the types of possible system failure(s) associated with the helicopter.
   b) Manufacturer's recommended procedures for dealing with the different types of system(s) failure.

Commercial PTS

Objective: To determine that the applicant—

1. Exhibits knowledge of the elements related to causes, indications, and pilot actions for various systems and equipment malfunctions.
2. Analyzes the situation and takes action appropriate to the helicopter used for the practical test.

Private Checklist FAA-S-8081-15

I.   PREFLIGHT PREPARATION
___ A. Certificates and documents
___ B. Airworthiness requirments
___ C. Weather information
___ D. Cross-country flight planning
___ E. National airspace system
___ F. Performance and limitations
___ G. Operation of systems
___ H. Aeromedical factors

II.   PREFLIGHT PROCEDURES
___ A. Preflight inspection
___ B. Cockpit management
___ C. Engine starting and rotor engagement
___ D. Before takeoff check

III.   AIRPORT AND HELIPORT OPERATIONS
___ A. Radio communications and ATC light signals
___ B. Traffic patterns
___ C. Airport/heliport runway, helipad, and taxiway signs, markings, and lighting

IV.   HOVERING MANEUVERS
___ A. Vertical takeoff and landing
___ B. Slope operations
___ C. Surface taxi
___ D. Hover taxi
___ E. Air taxi

V.   TAKEOFFS, LANDINGS, AND GO-AROUNDS
___ A. Normal and crosswind takeoff and climb
___ B. Normal and crosswind approach
___ C. Maximum performance takeoff and climb
___ D. Steep approach
___ E. Rolling takeoff
___ F. Confined area operations
___ G. Pinnacle/platform operations
___ H. Shallow approach and running roll-on landing
___ I. Go-around

VI.   PERFORMANCE MANEUVERS
___ A. Rapid deceleration
___ B. Straight in autorotation
___ C. 180° autorotation

VII.   NAVIGATION
___ A. Pilotage and dead reckoning
___ B. Radio navigation and radar services
___ C. Diversion
___ D. Lost procedures

VIII.   EMERGENCY OPERATIONS
___ A. Power failure at a hover
___ B. Power failure at altitude
___ C. Systems and equipment malfunctions
___ D. Settling-with-power
___ E. Low rotor RPM recovery
___ F. Antitorque system failure
___ G. Dynamic rollover
___ H. Ground resonance
___ I. Low G conditions
___ J. Emergency equipment and survival gear

IX.   NIGHT OPERATION
___ A. Night preparation

X.   POST-FLIGHT PROCEDURES
___ A. After landing and securing

Commercial Checklist FAA-S-8081-16

I.   PREFLIGHT PREPARATION
___ A. Certificates and documents
___ B. Airworthiness requirements
___ C. Weather information
___ D. Cross-country flight planning
___ E. National airspace system
___ F. Performance and limitations
___ G. Operation of systems
___ H. Aeromedical factors
___ I. Physiological aspects of night flying
___ J. Lighting and equipment for night flying

II.   PREFLIGHT PROCEDURES
___ A. Preflight inspection
___ B. Cockpit management
___ C. Engine starting and rotor engagement
___ D. Before takeoff check

III.   AIRPORT AND HELIPORT OPERATIONS
___ A. Radio communications and ATC light signals
___ B. Traffic patterns
___ C. Airport/heliport runway, heliport, and taxiway signs, markings, and lighting

IV.   HOVERING MANEUVERS
___ A. Vertical takeoff and landing
___ B. Slope operations
___ C. Surface taxi
___ D. Hover taxi
___ E. Air taxi

V.   TAKEOFFS, LANDINGS, AND GO-AROUNDS
___ A. Normal and crosswind takeoff and climb
___ B. Normal and crosswind approach
___ C. Maximum performance takeoff and climb
___ D. Steep approach
___ E. Rolling takeoff
___ F. Shallow approach and running/roll-on landing
___ G. Go-around

VI.   PERFORMANCE MANEUVERS
___ A. Rapid deceleration
___ B. Straight in autorotation
___ C. 180° autorotation
___ D. Approach and landing with simulated powerplant failure—multiengine helicopter

VII.   NAVIGATION
___ A. Pilotage and dead reckoning
___ B. Radio navigation and radar services
___ C. Diversion
___ D. Lost procedures

VIII.   EMERGENCY OPERATIONS
___ A. Power failure at a hover
___ B. Power failure at altitude
___ C. Systems and equipment malfunctions
___ D. Settling-with-power
___ E. Low rotor RPM recovery
___ F. Dynamic rollover
___ G. Ground resonance
___ H. Low G conditions
___ I. Emergency equipment and survival gear

IX.   SPECIAL OPERATIONS
___ A. Confined area operation
___ B. Pinnacle/platform operations

X.   POST-FLIGHT PROCEDURES
___ After landing and securing

Flight Instructor Checklist FAA-S-8081-7

I. FUNDAMENTALS OF INSTRUCTING
___ A. The learning process
___ B. Human behavior
___ C. The teaching process
___ D. Teaching methods
___ E. Critique and evaluation
___ F. Flight Instructor characteristics and responsibilities
___ G. Planning instructional activity

II. TECHNICAL SUBJECTS
___ A. Aeromedical factors
___ B. Visual scanning and collision avoidance
___ C. Use of distractions during flight training
___ D. Principles of flight
___ E. Helicopter flight controls
___ F. Helicopter weight and balance
___ G. Navigation and flight planning
___ H. Night operations
___ I. Regulations and publications
___ J. Airworthiness requirements
___ K. National airspace system
___ L. Logbook entries and certificate endorsements

III. PREFLIGHT PREPARATION
___ A. Certificates and documents
___ B. Weather information
___ C. Operation of systems
___ D. Performance and limitations

IV. PREFLIGHT LESSON ON A MANEUVER TO BE PERFORMED IN FLIGHT
___ A. Maneuver lesson

V. PREFLIGHT PROCEDURES
___ A. Preflight inspection
___ B. Single-pilot resource management
___ C. Engine starting and rotor engagement
___ D. Before takeoff check

VI. AIRPORT AND HELIPORT OPERATIONS
___ A. Radio communications and ATC light signals
___ B. Traffic patterns
___ C. Airport and heliport markings and lighting

VII. HOVERING MANEUVERS
___ A. Vertical takeoff and landing
___ B. Surface taxi
___ C. Hover taxi
___ D. Air taxi
___ E. Slope operation

VIII. TAKEOFFS, LANDINGS, AND GO-AROUNDS
___ A. Normal and crosswind takeoff and climb
___ B. Maximum performance takeoff and climb
___ C. Rolling takeoff
___ D. Normal and crosswind approach
___ E. Steep approach
___ F. Shallow approach and running/roll-on landing
___ G. Go-around
___ H. Approach and landing with simulated powerplant failure—multiengine helicopter

IX. FUNDAMENTALS OF FLIGHT
___ A. Straight-and-level flight
___ B. Level turns
___ C. Straight climbs and climbing turns
___ D. Straight descents and descending turns

X. PERFORMANCE MANEUVERS
___ A. Rapid deceleration
___ B. Straight-in autorotation
___ C. 180° autorotation

XI. EMERGENCY OPERATIONS
___ A. Power failure at a hover
___ B. Power failure at altitude
___ C. Settling-with-power
___ D. Low rotor RPM recovery
___ E. Anti-torque system failure
___ F. Dynamic rollover
___ G. Ground resonance
___ H. Low "G" conditions
___ I. Systems and equipment malfunctions
___ J. Emergency equipment and survival gear

XII. SPECIAL OPERATIONS
___ A. Confined area operation
___ B. Pinnacle/platform operation

XIII. POSTFLIGHT PROCEDURES
___ A. After landing and securing